Pieced Curves
So Simple

THE 6-MINUTE CIRCLE AND OTHER TIME-SAVING DELIGHTS

DALE FLEMING

C&T PUBLISHING

Publisher: Amy Marson

Editorial Director: Gailen Runge

Acquisitions Editor: Jan Grigsby

Editor: Cyndy Lyle Rymer

Technical Editor: Helen Y. Frost

Copyeditor/Proofreader: Wordfirm Inc.

Cover Designer: Kristen Yenche

Design Director/Book Designer: Kristen Yenche

Illustrator: Kirstie L. McCormick

Production Assistant: Kirstie L. McCormick

Photography: Quilts by Kathleen Bellesiles, Little Apple Studio; How-to photography by Luke Mulks

Photo Styling: Diane Pedersen

Published by C&T Publishing, Inc., P.O. Box 1456, Lafayette, California, 94549

Front cover: *Identity Crisis*

Back cover: (Clockwise) Details of *Just Circles*, *Handel's Water Music*, *Hearts*, *Hot Flash*, *Mondrian Waves*, and *Tuscan Sunflowers*

Library of Congress Cataloging-in-Publication Data

Fleming, Dale

  Pieced Curves So Simple: The 6-Minute Circle and Other Time-Saving Delights / Dale Fleming.

    p. cm.

  Includes bibliographical references and index.

  ISBN 1-57120-293-5 (paper trade)

  1. Machine quilting—Patterns. 2. Patchwork—Patterns. 3. Circle in art.

I. Title.

  TT835.F575 2005

  746.46—dc22

2004017072

Printed in China

10 9 8 7 6 5 4 3 2

ACKNOWLEDGMENTS

Little did I realize how many people would be helping and encouraging me when I considered writing a book. Shop owners, quilters, friends, and family—all had a part in helping create this book. Just as at the Academy Awards, I am unable to thank everyone, but I would like to mention certain people.

Thanks to the C&T Publishing family, who has worked so hard to bring this book to life.

Because I am dyslexic, I have several editors. The first is my sister, Diane Slater, who makes my nonsense sentences make sense. She made the writing part much more enjoyable. Rene Steinpress clarified the inital instructions, and Sally Swanson, Laura Nownes, and Janet Abbott gave the copy a final edit before I sent it off.

Kathleen Bellesiles of Little Apple Studio did a marvelous job with the quilt photography.

My testers Margaret Linderman, Freddy Moran, Anne Oldford, Rene Steinpress, and Angie Woolman were invaluable in working out the bugs in the projects and giving good advice.

My quilting friends produced quilts on very short notice: Jane Beatty, Brenda Colla, Emily Fleming, Lee Fowler, Dawn Guglielmino, Denise Killingsworth, Diana Mehrmann, Margaret Rice, and Vicki Wind.

DEDICATION

This book is dedicated to my family. The encouragement, expertise, and love of my children, Emily and Nicholas, have helped me grow. I am delighted to be their mother. My husband, Jerry, has always believed I can do anything, and his love has brought out the best in me. This book would not have happened without them.

SPECIAL THANKS

Diana McClun and Freddy Moran, who have been good friends and mentors and have encouraged me in my quilting endeavors

Laverne Edwards, who taught me to see how color really works and fine-tuned the sections on design and color

Christine Reite, a graphic artist who clarified my ideas, and created the graphics for the Color and Design Principles chapter

Pat Reite and her husband John, a master craftsman, who bail me out whenever I get stuck

Dr. Michael Slater, professor of communications at Colorado State University, and Denise Killingworth, an occupational therapist, helped me with effective information organization. Denise also does much of my handwork, is part of my critique group, and who never hesitates to say, "It doesn't work. Why don't you…?" Also her husband, Fitz Killingsworth, who explains the nuances of anything mechanical or computerized

Dawn Guglielmino, my weekly quilting partner, collaborator on many quilts, and yin to my yang. Dawn introduced me to quilting and made me write this book.

My parents Carmen and Gerald Borrmann, who encouraged me to experiment with fabric, dye, paint, and foods and allowed me to make some glorious messes as a child, which I have continued as an adult

My grandmother, Hettee Wade, who first taught me to sew and the joy of creativity

And last but not least, my family—my son Nicholas, who taught me computer basics; my daughter Emily, who helped refine the project; and my husband Jerry, who has supported me in every way.

Table of

Contents

The Essentials

This book is intended for adventurous souls who are open to trying new things. Whether you think of yourself as a traditional quiltmaker or a fabric artist, these techniques can simplify your cloth adventures.

Pinless Piecing uses glue rather than pins to hold fabric together while you sew. The instructions for the Six-Minute Circles (see page 26) explain the fundamentals of Pinless Piecing, and are the foundation for all the methods described in this book. The subsequent chapters and sidebars demonstrate various ways of using Pinless Piecing. Chapters 9 and 10 show how to use multiple methods in combination. Unpaper Piecing (see page 64) demonstrates how to use Pinless Piecing with unrelated techniques, while All Together Now (page 73) illustrates ways to combine the different skills you have learned. The piecing techniques are designed to increase speed and precision and to make difficult piecing easier. Although novices have successfully learned these techniques, students who have mastered the basic skills of quiltmaking probably will be able to progress more quickly.

Morning Coffee, 58" x 53", designed and pieced by Brenda Colla, Lodi, California, 2003; machine quilted by Victoria Simpson and Michelle Lingo, Galt, California.

Brenda successfully completed the background and border for this quilt in a class but couldn't decide how to finish the center. After she found a pattern for coffee cups and a coffeepot, she set them in during one afternoon. This sunny quilt now cheers her breakfast nook.

Because I tend to think of myself as a colorist first and a quilter second, I believe that an understanding of color theory and design principles not only helps solve problems, but also encourages the exploration of new ideas. Chapter 2, Color and Design Principles, explains the pigment and light theory color wheel on which I base my quilt color selections.

Each project and the accompanying quilt demonstrate a particular aspect of Pinless Piecing. Design elements, inspirations, and fabric choices are presented so you understand the reasons behind the choices. The projects build successively on previously introduced skills. Even if you decide you only want to learn techniques, without making any of the demonstration quilts, I suggest making a sample of each technique from every chapter or project.

Once you have learned a technique, reviewing the project illustrations will remind you how to use that method. If you run into trouble on a quilt that incorporates techniques from an earlier project, page numbers are listed to refer you to the initial discussion of those techniques.

Above all else, enjoy yourself and the journey.

MATERIALS AND EQUIPMENT

Every project refers back to the following list. Basic sewing supplies are used in all projects. For generic supplies, any brand will do. However, when supplies are specified by brand name (for example, Avery Removable Glue Stic), that product works best of all the different brands I have tried.

Basic Sewing Supplies 1–13

1. A good quality sewing machine. Unpaper Piecing (see page 64) requires a machine with a zigzag stitch throat plate.

2. Good quality sewing thread.

3. Sewing machine jeans/denim needles, size 80/12. This stiff needle will not bend sideways when sewing multiple layers of fabric.

4. 1/4" quilting foot and walking foot.

5. Pins. Flower-head pins are long and lie flat; fine glass-head pins can be ironed over without melting.

6. A clean iron and spray bottle.

 To clean your iron, use a wet scouring sponge with dish detergent and water on a cool iron.

7. Rotary cutters: one for fabric and one for paper. A crafts knife is optional.

8. Rotary cutting mat.

9. Assorted acrylic rulers: 6" x 24", 1" x 12", and square. Grab every size of square ruler you can find; it is much easier to square up wildly pieced blocks when you can see exactly where they end.

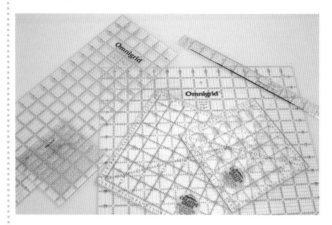

10. Fabric, paper, and fine-tip fabric scissors.

11. Seam ripper and fine-point tweezers.

12. Tapes. Blue 1"-wide Scotch Safe-Release Painters' masking tape makes putting "notes" on fabric easy. If the tape is ironed while on the fabric, no glue residue remains after it is peeled off. This tape also peels off cleanly from freezer paper and vellum. In addition, quilters' 1/8"- or 1/4"-wide masking tape is good for marking positions of blocks and quilting lines.

13. Colored pencils—white, turquoise, pink, and lime—for marking on fabric.

Pattern Supplies 14–18

14. Freezer paper for patterns. You can find this in quilt shops or in grocery stores next to the foil. One side of the paper has a shiny plastic coating that will temporarily bond to fabric with heat.

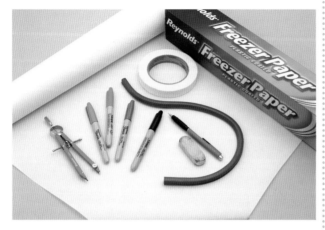

15. Vellum for drawing designs, available in rolls of various widths from art supply stores, as well as on the Internet at masterg.com. I buy the widest roll I can find, such as 42″ x 60′. Vellum is sturdy, withstands multiple erasures without ripping, and it is translucent so you can turn it over and see a good mirror image of your drawing. Tracing paper and poster paper can be substituted and are much less expensive, but the first tears very easily and the second is opaque.

16. Mechanical pencils, eraser, compass, flex curve, and other drawing tools.

17. Fine-point indelible ink pens: black, red, blue, and green, not microtip.

18. Fairly new, 1″-wide, tan masking tape. The lighter the masking tape, the less smell it will produce when you iron it.

Do NOT use disappearing purple glue sticks. The purple will reappear when you use the steam iron.

Pinless Piecing Supplies 19–25

19. Zipper sewing machine foot that allows you to adjust the needle $1/16$″ to the left of the outside edge of the foot, like the Pfaff. For example, the Singer Featherweight with a short-shank, adjustable narrow zipper foot works well. For Bernina and many other brands, an adapter is available that will make this generic adjustable foot fit your machine. If an adapter is not available for your machine, a regular zipper foot or an open-toed foot with a $1/4$″ opening (known as an embroidery foot) will work. For more options see Troubleshooting on page 29.

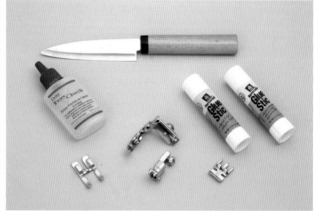

20. Two kinds of glue sticks: Avery Removable Glue Stic, 8g (buy several), and Avery Permanent Glue Stic, 8g (a full box). Avery glue is the firmest of the glue sticks and is of archival quality, which means it is acid-free and has no contaminants. My research indicates that this glue can be left in the quilt with no negative side effects. It is also water-soluble, so you can wash your finished quilt. If your glue stick is slightly mushy, put it in the refrigerator to firm it up. See All About Glue (page 30) for more information on glue sticks.

21. An inexpensive thin, dull paring knife to ease the glued fabric from the pattern. The knife must be thin enough to slide under the edge of the fabric but not sharp enough to cut into it. Dull the blade by rubbing it straight down on a rock; be sure to dull the point too.

22. A very firm design/ironing board. Next to your sewing machine, place a board that is hard enough for you to create a very sharp crease with your iron but that can also be pierced with pins for holding your composition in place while you work. There are several ways to make this work area.

The easiest is to purchase a Cushioned Quilter's Square'n Blocker (model JT 705, 24" x 18", *without* the cutting mat on the back) made by June Tailor. It has both hard (the back) and soft ironing surfaces. Pins will stick into the hard surface side to hold your work in position. Any store that carries June Tailor supplies can order these; they are also available on the web at www.junetailor.com, or by calling 1-800-844-5400.

For a larger work surface I use a 30" x 30" piece of fiberboard painted on one side, also called white-faced Celotex. Fiberboard can be purchased at a lumberyard, possibly even in the size you need. Cover the painted side of the board with a thin layer of 100% cotton batting, then a layer of white cotton fabric, and staple or tape both layers to the fiberboard. This perfect work surface is hard enough to create a sharp crease, while allowing pins to insert easily. Unfortunately, large squares of fiberboard break easily, so this work surface is not very portable.

Another option is to make a quick substitute for fiberboard by using a 1/2"-thick wood board covered with a layer of cotton batting and one layer of cotton fabric. However, because pins used for positioning fabric do not penetrate the wood, the more complex methods described in this book are a challenge.

23. A soft terrycloth towel to soften the hard ironing surface when pressing the seam in a different direction and for the final ironing.

24. Scrap white cotton fabric at least 24" x 24" to cover your work surface when you apply glue to the individual units and extra to clean off excess glue on the edges and front of a unit.

25. Dritz Fray Check, a fabric glue that prevents raveling.

Unpaper Piecing Supplies 26–28

26. Mid- to heavy-weight (coat or jacket) fusible interfacing such as Pellon, which is heavy enough to hold its shape when fabrics are sewn to it and substantial enough for a wing needle to punch visible holes.

27. Sewing machine wing needle, size 120/19. This needle can be found where embroidery sewing machines are sold. A wide throat plate is also required with this type of needle.

28. Stapler and staple remover and microtip permanent marker.

DESIGN WALLS

I use a design wall or board for every quilt I make. A design wall is nothing more than an area to hang a quilt in progress so you can stand back and critique it. Fabric looks very different from afar. Colors may appear to blend, disappear, gray, turn to mush, or take over the whole quilt.

Foam-core boards, curtains, or flannel pinned to a wall work well. I like gridded flannel because it helps with block placement. Once the pieces of the quilt are on the design wall, use a reducing glass, digital camera, or Polaroid camera to review the design and look for problem areas. When viewed upright in a small format, the basic elements of your design often become clear.

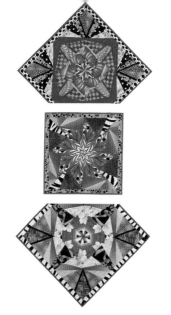

chapter two

Color and Design Principles

COLOR WHEEL

Many quilters are intimidated by the color wheel and the terminology surrounding it. I can empathize. Over the years, I've seen more than a dozen different color wheels. Some are based on the colors in light, others on pigments, and few seem to portray colors that appear in nature. I too had difficulty using color wheels—until I met Laverne Edwards.

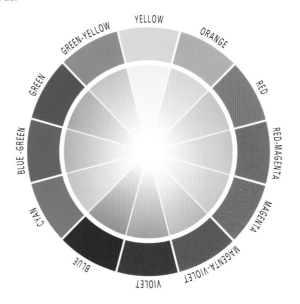

Laverne is an incredible teacher and friend who taught at the Rudolf Schaffer School of Design and the California College of Arts in Oakland, California. In her 1992 color theory class, I was introduced to a color wheel, which originated in the Bauhaus movement of 1920s Germany and incorporates both the colors of light and those used in industry.

Color is one of the most important aspects of quilting. People love the colors in fabrics but often are uncertain about how to put them together in a quilt. When choosing a fabric color palette, do not be a slave to the color wheel. Instead, let the wheel nudge you into trying different and new combinations of colors or rely on it to solve problems when your intuition is not working. Find the colors you are using on the color wheel, and then look at the color relationships of harmony, balance, contrast, and continuity to see what is missing from your composition.

COLOR VOCABULARY

When designers and artists talk about color, they describe its qualities with terms that mean the same to anyone who works with color and design. The precision of the following terms will help you understand how and why certain color combinations work. A helpful exercise is to pull fabrics that demonstrate each concept. If you handle the material, you will not forget the concept. The defined terms are in italics, followed by a sample demonstration of their proper use.

Hue is the precise term for a color found on the color wheel. For example, the color pink is a magenta hue.

Value refers to a light/dark comparison. If the design in a quilt does not stand out, check whether the values of the colors being used are too close to one another. If it's hard to tell the values, you can use a photocopier. Adjust the copier to the photo setting and photocopy the fabrics in black and white. Value is the most important element in making a design work.

1–9 gray scale

Intensity or *saturation* suggests how much hue is perceived and how bright the color is. Orange is a more saturated color than gold. If a color appears too overwhelming, a color of less intensity will often work; it is the same color, just not as intense. Create less saturated colors by using tints, tones, or shades of the color.

A full orange and gold of the same value

Tint is a hue with white added to it. Azure is a tint of cyan.

Tints of cyan

Tone is a hue with gray added to it. Another word to describe tone is "dull." Due to the availability of dyes for industry use, it is difficult to find a pure hue of blue or green in cotton fabric; most blue or green fabric colors are tones. A tone will make its complementary color stand out, but it will not stand out to the same degree itself. Tones are useful if you want some subtlety in your quilt; for example, tones add mist or fog to a hue, and neutral tones add warmth or coolness to a hue.

Tones of cyan

Shade is a hue with black added to it. Teal is a shade of turquoise. If you want a very dark color but don't want to use black, use a shade. I call these "black wanna-bes" (see page 21). A shade can add subtlety to a quilt because it carries the mystique of black while altering the appearance and retaining the darker value.

Shades of cyan

Color-base and *common neutrals* are bridging fabrics, or fabrics that appear to be brown, tan, or gray. If three or more hues are mixed together, they create a flat, colorless mass that, in small quantities, makes all the colors interrelate. In quilting, unlike in painting, you cannot mix one color into others to create a common neutral. Therefore, use bridging fabrics, which have bits of many other colors, to pull a variety of colors together. If, when you stand way back, the bridging fabrics appear gray, tan, or brown, they are a common neutral. If they still have an identifiable overall color, they are a color-base neutral. Every quilt I make includes some of these indispensable fabrics because they allow odd color combinations to come together and play nicely. Dots, plaids, and florals are often found in this role.

Bridging fabrics

Cool colors are usually the hues from visible green to violet magenta, and those from yellow through the oranges to red are considered warm. *Hot Flash* (page 73) has a primarily cool border and figure, though the background is HOT!

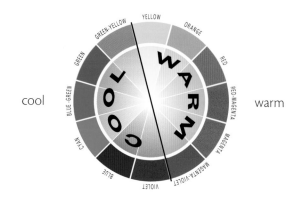

Warm and cool

Simultaneous contrast is the effect noncomplementary colors have on one another. Every time you add a color to your quilt, the dynamics change. A yellow-orange placed next to a lime green will look very orange, but next to red it will look more yellow. Colors will look warmer, cooler, brighter, duller, or like a different color entirely depending on their placement. Josef Albers, a twentieth-century German-American painter, spent years exploring simultaneous contrast (see page 17).

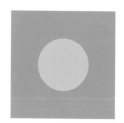 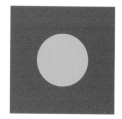

Gold yellow/lime   *Gold yellow/red*

COLOR HARMONIES

Understanding how colors relate to one another is useful for quilt design and composition. If your colors don't seem just right, note where they are on the color wheel and consider what you might adjust.

Monochromatic is a color palette created with one hue. Tints, tones, shades, and many values of this hue are all included. A misty morning in the Blue Ridge Mountains might evoke this palette.

Blue

Analogous refers to three or more closely related colors. When working with fabric, you are at the mercy of the dye manufacturers, and the exact color you want may not be available. However, if you use a mixture of closely related hues, you can create the illusion of the hue

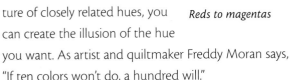

Reds to magentas

you want. As artist and quiltmaker Freddy Moran says, "If ten colors won't do, a hundred will."

Complementary colors are the two colors opposite each other on the color wheel. When complementary colors are placed next to each other, the edge between them visually vibrates, and they both stand out. Op art uses this phenomenon extensively.

Complementary colors

Split complementaries are complementary colors that include the two colors on either side of one of the colors. If you want to make violet really pop but don't have the right yellow, fabrics with butter-yellow and lime will make the violet stand out. A carefully selected group of analogous colors will have the same effect.

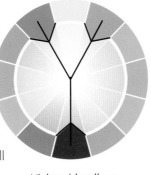

Violet with yellows

Triad harmonies are three colors evenly spaced around the color wheel that can create harmony in a composition. If red threatens to take over your quilt, add green or violet. The red will no longer dominate; instead, it will sing along.

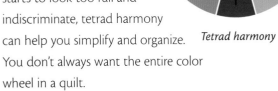

Triad harmony

Tetrad harmonies describe four colors around the color wheel: either four evenly spaced colors or two sets of complementary colors. When your color palette pile starts to look too full and indiscriminate, tetrad harmony can help you simplify and organize. You don't always want the entire color wheel in a quilt.

Tetrad harmony

UNITY

Unity is that wonderful quality that makes all the parts of the quilt look like they belong together. As you design, consider these principles so the colors and shapes will work well together.

Balance and proportion in color are achieved by using different quantities of color to keep colors from either taking over a quilt or disappearing. Warm and light colors appear to advance against cool and dark colors, which seem to recede. The greater the contrast in color and value, the greater the appearance of depth. If you have equal amounts of yellow and violet, the yellow will appear to expand, and the quilt will feel as though it is mostly yellow.

As you begin to design and play with fabric possibilities, you need to be aware of the relationships of the colors you plan to use to ensure that you achieve balance. In *Charles Was Having Tea When a Luau Happened* (page 24), the 1/4" strip of screaming yellow stands out between the black and magenta and makes the 1/2" black strip appear the same size as the 1/4" yellow strip. If these two proportions were reversed, the thicker yellow strip would take over the quilt, and the thinner black strip would disappear. As you work on the design or sewing of a quilt, don't hesitate to change the fabric shapes and sizes if the color warrants it.

Visual balance refers to the placement of shapes and colors on a quilt and the relation to each other. This relation is what creates symmetry. These placements are also called "focal points." Balance can be radial, symmetrical, or asymmetrical.

Radial symmetry means that the pattern emerges from the center. Think of the Lone Star, Sunburst, or Dahlia pattern.

Sunburst drawing

Symmetry is when a block or quilt is folded in half and each side of the axis, the line around which the design is formed, is a mirror image of the other half. In her book *Symmetry*, Ruth McDowell explores seventeen possible symmetries of a block. The repetition of color and shape makes these quilts cohesive and balanced, which may be why most traditional quilts are symmetrical. The memory blocks in *Diana's Memory Block* are symmetrical; the shapes are the same no matter which way the quilt is turned.

Diana's Memory Block,
Dale Fleming

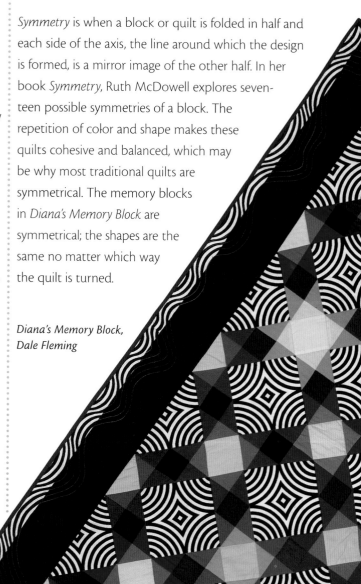

Asymmetrical designs use different sizes, shapes, or colors to create a sense of balance. Look for an imaginary axis line or point around which the composition appears to be balanced. Think, for example, of an Alexander Calder mobile. Note that the numerous smaller shapes balance the fewer larger ones. Look at how the shapes are spaced. Calder was a master of complex compositions that are visually and physically balanced.

Although this is extremely simplistic, here's a rule of thumb: Look for a triangle. Many works of art have an imaginary triangle. This triangle leads the eye by balancing the visual "weight" and spreading the objects of interest so the composition doesn't feel lopsided. Of course, triangles come in many shapes and sizes.

Alexander Calder, Lone Yellow, 1961. Metal, 34" x 84", San Francisco Museum of Modern Art. Gift of Jean Lipman from the Lipman Family Collection. © Estate of Alexander Calder/ Artists Rights Society (ARS), New York.

Rhythm refers to visual rhythm, which requires the repetition of a design element at certain intervals. When repeated throughout the quilt, visual rhythm leads to *continuity*. Traditional quilts often consist of one pattern repeated in a predictable fashion, with little change from unit to unit. The patterns are easy to discern, even in a quilt with a complex structure. When dissimilar units are put together, certain elements or shapes need to be repeated to substitute for the missing predictable pattern.

The long lines in *Handel's Water Music* (page 61) create the necessary repetition in this quilt. The rhythm of *Claire in a Field of Lupines* (page 25) is created by boldly shaped lupines in various sizes and by the blue inner borders, which create a visual figure eight. The splashes of gold lend further continuity and help move the viewer's eye through the composition. Quilting lines are often used to enhance a quilt's rhythm.

Rest is a graphic design term that refers to the part of the design that is not "busy." Compositions need a place with a break in the activity so the eye can recognize the separate elements of the design instead of seeing a jumble of texture and color. Common neutrals—dull colors, black, and white—sashing, or gridlines, and the background or negative space all create visual rest.

Positive space refers to a shape. The circle is a positive space.

Negative space refers to the area surrounding the shape. Negative space is often referred to as background.

Although these basic definitions provide a good grounding in the subjects of color and design, color or design classes are a good way to develop your eye. It also helps to read as much as you can. Some of my favorite books are listed in the Bibliography (page 80). The best sources for design and art books are museums and college bookstores, but because design books can be expensive, look through a book before you buy it. And remember, if you want a purple cow, make a purple cow—it's your quilt!

chapter three

Inspiration

OR, HOW DID YOU COME UP WITH THAT?

The development of a quilt, from the first glimmer of an idea to the last stitch, can take a long time. Because getting started can be difficult, here are some ways artists can spark the process.

OBSERVE

You don't need to make a pictorial quilt for nature to be an inspiration. My greatest source of inspiration is the world around me. On my daily walks, I notice the wind blowing ripples on a grassy hillside, light shining through leaves, fences, gravel strewn across the path, wood stacked in a pile, and doors and windows on a building. These observations make me more aware of patterns, unusual color combinations, and shapes. Many of these patterns would make a wonderful quilt layout.

Plants are a source of unusual color combinations in which surprise colors pop up. One corner of my garden has become a favorite color combination: orange, lilac, scarlet, and magenta.

Sea of truffles

Look around you every day for sources of inspiration. One of these days, the combination of balls, squares, and rectangular-shaped chocolate truffles spread across my counter will inspire me to make a quilt.

RESEARCH

Seek out visual experiences. Museum exhibits of all kinds will show you how other cultures and artists have explored the use of colors and shapes. Georgia O'Keeffe used large, bold shapes with unusual color combinations, inspired by the deserts of the Southwest. Bridget Riley, a celebrated op artist, is all about motion and movement. Andrew Goldsworthy, who works with found objects, makes you reassess how you may have looked at shapes and color in nature in the past.

The work of Josef Albers has been a huge influence on me; his studies of the interactions of color are endlessly fascinating. The color values in his paintings are so perfectly balanced that a halo effect is created. In his multihued color study painting, his choice of color placement changes the perceived color. The lesson is: It is not only the color you use, but also the color you put next to it, that makes the color you perceive. Every quilt I have made explores the concept of *simultaneous contrast.*

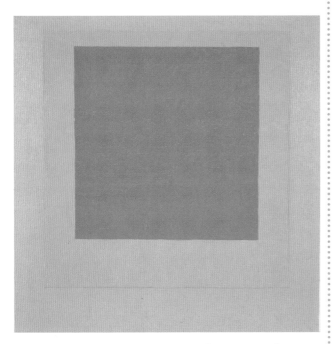

Josef Albers, Homage to the Square: "Confident," 1954, oil on masonite, 24" x 24". San Francisco Museum of Modern Art; gift of Mrs. Anni Albers and The Josef Albers Foundation; © Josef and Anni Albers Foundation/Artists Rights Society (ARS), New York. Thicker orange and blue lines are at the bottom of squares within squares.

Piet Mondrian is another artist who has influenced me. His post-1920 paintings are compositions that study the balance of colors and rectangles in an irregular grid. Each painting has a rhythm that plays across the surface.

Piet Mondrian, Composition with Red, Yellow, and Blue, 1935-1942, oil on canvas, 39³/₄" x 20¹/₈". San Francisco Museum of Modern Art; purchased through a gift of Phyllis Wattis; © Mondrian/ Holtzman Trust, c/o Beeldrecht/ Artists Rights Society (ARS), New York.

I have taught and explored the concepts introduced by Mondrian's paintings since 1997, when I started a fiftieth anniversary quilt for my parents and decided to try a less symmetrical grid to make the keepsake quilt more unusual. If you make a quilt with blocks and settings of varying sizes, remember that the gridlines, or sashing, are as important as the blocks themselves because they impart rhythm to the composition. Quilts in this book that show a Mondrian influence are *Hearts* (page 40), *Guatemalan Square Dance* (page 23), and *Mondrian Waves* (page 69).

For additional research, go to quilt shows and analyze the quilts. What do you see first? What message do you get? What do you like and dislike? You can learn from other quilters' successes and mistakes. Read poetry. What do you visualize? Listen to music and dream. *Handel's Water Music* (page 61) was inspired by that piece of music.

Begin with your observations, then analyze and consider how they relate to you and how they might be translated into quilt designs. Examine small moments for the beginnings of an idea.

EXPERIMENT

Try something new and be willing to experiment. Take classes that are growth experiences and that require you to stretch yourself. Fusing, collage, and painting are all variations of quilting. Your experiment may not be your favorite medium, but it might open up new ways of thinking and expand your practical knowledge of design, color, and materials. Play with your fabric, making piles of fabric with different amounts of color showing. Look at block patterns. My favorite source is Barbara Brackman's *Encyclopedia of Pieced Quilt Patterns*. Make experimental blocks and try changing lines or colors. Experiments that don't work can always be recycled, so no effort is ever wasted. The generation of ideas is exponential; the more things you try, the more possibilities you will see.

JUST START SEWING

I always have "no-brainer" quilts in the works—quick, fun quilts that do not require many design decisions. *Dancing People* is a good example. When I am at a loss for an idea or stuck on a concept quilt, it often helps to sew on a no-brainer quilt. The simple act of sewing a nonchallenging project often allows ideas to surface and solutions to come to you.

David Bayles and Ted Orland tell a story in their book *Art and Fear* that supports the "just do it" approach. A synopsis of the story is: Some art students were divided into two groups. The first group was told they would be graded on the number of pots they made. Quality didn't count, just numbers. The second group was told they only had to make one pot, but it had to be perfect. The first group threw hundreds of pots, many of them ugly and mis-shapen. The second group read books, debated what a perfect pot would look like, and then made their single pot. When, in the end, the single pot was compared with the final pots of the mass producers, the mass producers' final pots had more grace and beauty than the single pot.

Open your eyes and take a good look at the world around you. Explore new ideas and techniques, and then just start sewing.

First Quilt, 54" x 68", designed and machine pieced by Emily Fleming, Davis, California; machine quilted by Lee Fowler, Portland, Oregon, 2003.
My daughter, Emily, made her first quilt for a good friend's baby. When she was home one weekend, between shopping and laundry, I taught her how to quilt. She found the circles easier to sew than the triangles, though now she is hooked and plans to make more quilts.

Dancing People, 55" x 66", designed and pieced by Dale Fleming, quilted by Lee Fowler, 2003.

Critiquing Your Work

Critique your work at every stage of the quiltmaking process. The key to a productive, positive critique is to know what sorts of questions to ask. Regard the critiquing process as an opportunity to learn how well your quilt expresses what you want it to say.

First, take a break. Whether you have pulled fabric, made a drawing, sewed pieces together, or arranged blocks, the advice remains the same. Leave it alone for several hours or days, let your subconscious work on it, and, when you begin again, look at it with a fresh eye.

Begin with the following helpful guidelines for an effective critique.

1. Ask yourself what you see. Is the first thing you see what you want to jump out? What do you like or not like about that prominent element? Why? Analyze the strengths of a quilt rather than just its problems.

2. Ask other people what they see. I call this "quilting by committee," and it can be a lot of fun. After working on something for a long time, most people tend to see whatever was the most demanding, which may not be the most eye-catching element. You don't have to follow the advice others give you, but their advice will tell you how other people perceive your work.

3. When something jumps out at you visually, do you like it? If all you see is bright pink fabric, consider some alternatives. If necessary, refer to Chapter 2, Color and Design Principles.

• Try taking out the color. If you like the overall effect better with it in, then it probably needs to stay.

• If you decide you like the color but it seems too bright, try substituting a different value, tint, tone, or shade.

• If you like the color but feel that it draws too much attention to one part of the quilt, add more of it in another area for balance or add some analogous fabrics to give it some friends.

• If you like the color but don't want to add more of it in other areas, add the triad colors, which in this example would be turquoise and yellow. The pink will still be strong, but the impact will be more harmonious.

4. Can you see the shapes you want to see? If not, check the values of the foreground and background and the amount of contrast. If a design is not working, it is often because of a problem with the value.

5. Is there a place for the eye to rest? Stand back and view the quilt from afar. Use a camera or reducing glass.

6. Does the quilt feel balanced? If your eye always goes to one area first, is that where you want it to go? Does the quilt have a focal point? Putting all the yellows in one spot will usually attract the eye; so consider whether you have created a triangle for the eye to follow. Think of your quilt as a mobile in which the weights are balanced.

7. Is there rhythm and continuity? Do elements repeat themselves throughout the quilt so they look like they belong together? Is the repeated element a shape or color? Identify the elements that make your quilt cohesive.

These are just some of the questions you should ask yourself about your quilt, not just once, but many times over the course of its creation. The questions are the same whether you are making a traditional quilt or an art quilt. A critique is a conversation with a new friend; listen so you hear what is being said.

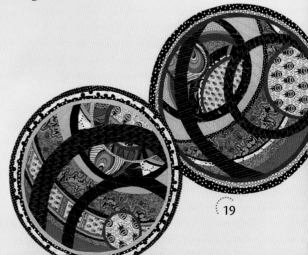

chapter four

Fabric

Quilts just beg to be touched. People love the soft drape and sensuous texture of fibers. I admit that quilting allows me to collect fabrics that even I couldn't possibly wear or put in my home: loud prints, dots, stripes, wild ethnic prints. But with so many choices and so little room to store it all, what should you buy?

First and most importantly, buy good-quality fabric. A quilt that falls apart or bleeds color is a complete waste of time and money. Most of my fabric is 100% cotton because it is easy to work with and sturdy. However, I also have silk, rayon, and the occasional shirt, tablecloth, or tie.

TO WASH OR NOT TO WASH

Prewash all your fabric. Some of the more unusual fabrics from around the world have been in the presence of strange chemicals. Washing also helps eliminate the excess dye for which certain brands of fabric, and most ethnic fabrics, are notorious. Wash these fabrics with Synthrapol, a chemical that helps remove excess dye from fabric. Prewashing also helps shrink the fabric. Many fabrics shrink to different degrees. By prewashing, you can use synthetic interfacing, hand-dyes, rayons, and silk in the same quilt without fear.

Another reason to prewash is that the Pinless Piecing method uses a steam iron in the last step. Steam ironing will shrink any fabric that is inclined to do so, so it is a good idea to ensure that all shrinkage has occurred before you start a new project.

QUANTITY

The decision of how much fabric to buy is directly related to the size of both your pocketbook and your storage space. My husband is sure that if I make a quilt a week for the next 100 years, I would use all of my stash. Without apologies, I doubt it. My mammoth collection ensures I have all the choices I could ever need, and I'm constantly adding to it.

Color availability is cyclical. Each year, manufacturers and buyers decide what colors are "in" and produce fabric, furniture, and decorative items in those selected colors. Also, because the vast majority of dyes are made with chemicals, new ones are constantly being developed, whereas some old ones may be outlawed for environmental reasons. This year's colors may no longer be available next season. What's more, you may not see that particular color again for years, or possibly never again.

I usually buy at least a half to a full yard of fabric, which enables me to cut strips from one end of the fabric and shapes from the other end. It gives me enough to experiment with the fabric, as well as enough left over to make a quilt.

BUILDING A FABRIC PANTRY

What basic necessities should you absolutely include in your fabric collection without having so much you have to rent a warehouse?

Black "wanna-bes" are very dark colors that read as black, indigo, or navy. Multiples of black in quilts impart a hidden texture and suggest shapes rather than just being unrelenting black. Many of these wanna-bes are shades (see page 12).

Black-and-white prints are valuable for their very graphic nature and high value change. The white adds sparkle and the black imparts drama.

Light values with texture can be hard to find, but when added to a quilt they enhance other colors and help them stand out. The wrong side of a printed fabric can be a great source for lights. Fabrics that look good on the back as well as the front are like free fabric: a two-for-one deal!

Geometrics, such as dots, grids, and stripes, add dimension and can act as a unifying element. Dots give visual texture without adding another shape. Grids, such as checkerboards, hexagons, and plaids, don't compete as shapes but do add strong horizontal and vertical elements. Stripes can be used to direct the eye to certain focal points or other important elements.

Bridging fabrics visually tie different colors together. You may not love these fabrics individually, but they work wonderfully with other fabrics. Before you buy, give it the "30-foot" test. Stand at least 30 feet away and consider what color is communicated. Bridging fabrics are the color-base and common neutrals (page 12).

Big, bold prints are prima donnas that can stump many quilters, but they are also infinitely attractive and dominant. They make a distinct statement and set the tone for the quilt. Cut them up for a unifying print that isn't repetitive.

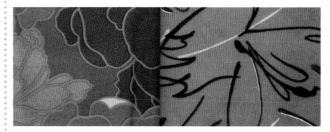

Just because! Buy a fabric just because you find it beautiful. If you can't find a way to use it as part of a design, it can go on the back of a quilt. After all, quilting is just an excuse to wallow in the texture and color of fabric.

Ethnic prints, such as batiks or Japanese, Australian, and African fabrics, have a distinctive style and feel that can set the tone of a quilt. The colors and patterns are a little different from commercial fabrics; as a result, these prints can impart interest to your more common fabrics and stretch your analogous color grouping.

In each of these "pantry" categories, look for fabrics with different print scales and think about how they will look when they are cut up. Busy little background prints tend to clutter your pantry, so buy those for each quilt project only as the need arises. Such prints are always available and give the quilt a contemporary feel if bought recently.

ESTABLISHING A MOOD

Colors evoke a wide variety of feelings, but different cultural traditions may perceive individual colors differently. In Asia, for example, white is associated with death, whereas in Western culture it is associated with weddings. In India, wedding saris are red, while red is a traditional Christmas color in the West. Even without these sentimental associations, color can create moods. Many people feel passion and energy around red or a soothing coolness when surrounded by blues and greens. As you select fabric, be sure to stand back to see if your color selections create the feeling for which you are striving.

Novelty fabrics, such as hearts, stars, food, cowboys, or any number of kitschy things, can be especially meaningful. If you have a special feeling for a certain item, collect it and use it in your quilts.

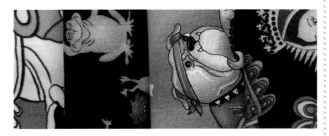

Reading good books on the subject may also help get you started. The interesting *Designers' Guide to Color* series illustrates classic combinations of colors from around the world. However, personal observations of and reactions to color may be the best and most reliable arbiter of color-oriented taste. For example, at an exciting carnival, what colors do you notice? I visualize black, white, and very intense, vibrantly flashy, hot colors. Now picture yourself sitting in a peaceful garden listening to birds; you probably see harmonious shades of green, with perhaps some elusive sparkles of color. When you tune in to your environment, you observe different mood spots. A book might help you clarify your ideas, but color response is so subjective that you would do well to look within yourself first.

Carnival   *A peaceful garden*

Make Your Own Fabric: Stripping

If you can't buy it or dye it, then strip it. *Stripping* is a time-honored method that quilters use to create a texture or color. It is also an excellent way to create a color-base or common neutral. Stripping consists of cutting a variety of fabrics into strips of different widths and then sewing them together. For *Hot Flash* (page 73), I used stripping to create a "hot" background, whereas I used stripping to create the texture of the leaves for *Tahoe Blue, Autumn* (page 67). Many people will sew strips in a very random manner and enjoy the surprise of the finished piece. I prefer more control because I have specific ideas about the appearance of the finished fabric. When stripping, I always put in little zingers of white, very bright, or very dark colors using strips between 1/8" and 1/2" wide.

Finished stripped fabric

Guatemalan Square Dance, 50½" x 47½", designed and pieced by Dawn Guglielmino; quilted by Lee Fowler, 2003.

Tip

Use a walking foot to prevent the strips from developing a curve as you sew. When sewing ¼" and ½" strips, the adjacent seam will often push the foot askew, so the seam will no longer be ¼". A walking foot, however, will ride up on a seam and continue to stitch straight.

CREATING A COLOR PALETTE

My inspiration for a new quilt is usually a combination of fabric and ideas. I start with an inspirational fabric, pull out samples of each color, and lay them out during the initial selection.

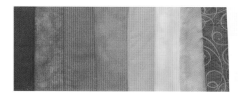

Then the hunt is on to find prints in a variety of scales that go with the identified colors. Look for different color values or analogous, complementary, or neutral colors—anything that might look good together. In the example, note the different values of green with the analogous colors of yellow to magenta. Also, look for colors that are *not* in the inspirational fabric. The blue stripe is complementary to the oranges and reds. Before the next stage of selection, remove those fabrics that exactly match the colors of the inspirational fabric.

The next step is to look for fabrics that work with your second selection of fabric. Look at the different color harmonies to see whether any combinations might add sparkle. Perhaps some of those fabrics that perfectly

matched the inspirational fabric should go back in. However, be sure to limit yourself to only a few perfectly matched fabrics, or your quilt will be very predictable. This is a chance to really think about what kind of mood you want to create and the best way to create that mood. I added more color-base neutrals at this time. I wanted more energy, so I replaced the calm gray floral with the stronger gray geometric. Also, black-and-white materials give the design more vibration. Notice how the black-and-white waves suggest motion.

For the final palette, a shot of intense yellow added more zip. This fabric collection offered many choices for creating a quilt.

Charles Was Having Tea When a Luau Happened was made with these fabrics. I planned a quiet tropical retreat, but as I pulled the fabrics and became more excited, the mood changed, and I wanted the quilt to be more like a party.

Charles Was Having Tea When a Luau Happened, 56" x 56", designed, pieced, and quilted by Dale Fleming, 2003.

Painless, Pinless Piecing: The Six-Minute Circle

Pinless Piecing evolved because I was desperate to find an easier way to create curves. I had taken classes that taught many methods to piece curves, and I learned many useful techniques. However, all the techniques were tedious. In 2000, as I was sitting next to a woman who was playing around with spray glue for appliqué, I wondered what would happen if glue were used a little differently. I then took a class from Ruth McDowell, designed *Claire in a Field of Lupines,* and used adhesives to sew the quilt. Several years later, after much experimentation and research, I have an easy, precise method for machine piecing curves.

chapter five

Pinless Piecing uses glue rather than pins to hold fabric together while you sew. It is fast and creates exact results with minimal effort. When a project described in this book says to use Pinless Piecing, follow the steps as described for the Six-Minute Circle (page 26); a quick summation of the steps is also provided on page 30.

Claire in a Field of Lupines, 62" x 34", Dale Fleming, 2001.

MAKE SAMPLES!

As you read the following chapters, consider making a small sample of each technique. The basic procedure—The Six-Minute Circle—is the foundation that everything else is built upon. Angles are added in Chapter 6, Tips and Cleavage (page 34). Several ways of using Pinless Piecing with patterns are shown in Chapter 7, Every Way to Play With Patterns (page 43), starts with following a pattern exactly, then adding details as you sew, and ending with collage. Convex (rounded outward) and concave (rounded inward) curves are explored in Chapter 8, Sinuous Curves (page 57). In Chapter 9 Pinless Piecing is also combined with an unrelated technique, Unpaper Piecing (page 64). Chapter 10, All Together Now (page 73), offers another example of using multiple techniques and demonstrates how to adapt Pinless Piecing to create your own designs.

Each technique is broken down into easy-to-follow steps. Even after you have completed a circle, point, or curve, continue to use the illustrations and photos in each section as quick how-to reminders.

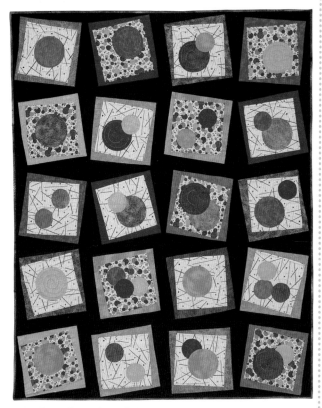

Simple Circles, 43" x 54", designed and machine pieced by Dawn Guglielmino, Walnut Creek, California; machine quilted by Victoria Simpson and Michelle Lingo, Galt, California, 2003. This is a variation of Just Circles that Dawn made in just 2 days.

THE SIX-MINUTE CIRCLE

Quilters have a love/hate relationship with circles. Circles and curves in nature inspire us, and we want to reproduce them in our own designs. Unfortunately, sewing circles can be a challenge. Sewing by hand takes a lot of time, while sewing by machine often leads to a series of short jerky lines rather than a smooth circle. As a result, quilters often avoid circles and curves, even if the shape is necessary to create the desired quilt. Making circles is the most basic of the Pinless Piecing skills. Once you have prepared your fabric and cut out your patterns, it takes only six minutes to complete a perfect circle. There are a number of circle quilt books on the market; one of the best is *Circle Play* by Reynola Pakusich. Once you learn the Six-Minute Circle method, any circle quilt can be made faster.

How-To's of Circles

1. To make a circle pattern, layer 2 squares of freezer paper so both shiny sides face down. Fuse the pieces together using a dry iron. Iron from the middle of the freezer paper to the edges to avoid bubbles. Draw the circle on freezer paper, allowing a 1" margin around the circle (for example, a 4" circle in a 6" square). Cut out the circle with paper scissors or a crafts knife. The square with the hole is the negative space pattern; the circle is the positive part of the pattern.

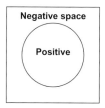

Step 1: *Freezer paper pattern*

To make a precisely placed circle—for example, in the center of the block—cut the freezer paper to the block size with the seam allowance added. Cut the circle exactly in the center of the paper block.

 If you are making many circles, a Fiskars circle cutter is a great tool to have on hand!

2. With the shiny side down, place the negative space pattern on the wrong side of your background fabric. Use a dry iron to fuse the pattern to the fabric.

Step 2: Iron pattern to background fabric.

3. Cut out the fabric on the inside of the circle, leaving at least a ½" seam allowance. Clip the seam allowance to ⅛" from the pattern. The frequency of clips depends on the tightness of the curve. The clipped seam, which I call the "fringe," needs to fold smoothly over the edge of the pattern with the minimum number of clippings.

 Do not clip too closely to the pattern, or you will have a hole on the front of your quilt.

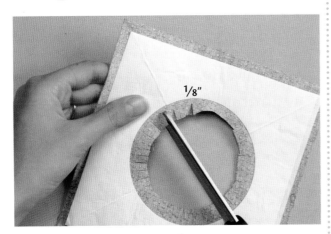

Step 3: Cut and clip to within ⅛" of pattern.

4. Use Avery Removable Glue Stic around the opening in the paper pattern. Let the removable glue dry for at least 1 minute until it becomes tacky. If you are using Avery Permanent Glue Stic, use just enough glue to tack down the clipped seam; excess glue makes it hard to peel off the pattern later. Use your finger or the tip of your iron to fold and press the clipped seam over the edge of the pattern. Use a dry iron to press the seam.

 Remember the "Glue Rule": Go lightly with the glue on paper, heavily with the permanent glue on the fabric.

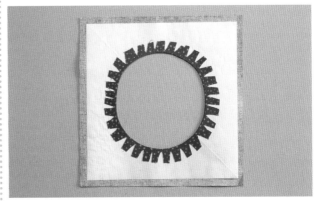

Step 4: Tack the clipped seam to the pattern.

 Use removable glue for the first tack, and a dot of permanent glue for any stray pieces.

5. Place the protective cotton cloth on your work surface. Generously apply Avery permanent glue on the edge of the clipped seam. The band of glue should be approximately ½" wide and should extend from the folded edge outward.

Step 5: Add a band of glue.

6. Use a cotton rag to wipe off any excess glue from the front of the folded edge. If you are not wiping glue blobs off the edge, you are probably not adding enough glue.

7. Place the glued side of the background fabric onto the right side of a square of the circle fabric. Adjust the background fabric over the circle fabric until it is positioned correctly. Finger press. Turn over and use a dry iron on the back until the glue is dry.

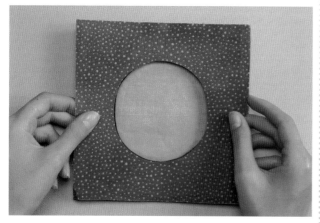

Step 7: Position background on circle fabric.

8. To remove the pattern from the fabric, peel the fabric from the shiny side of the pattern first. From the front, put your fingertip between the pattern and the seam. Use your fingertip to peel the paper away from the seam, sliding your finger from the fold outward. If you have done it correctly, the paper will pop right off. If not, use a dull paring knife to lift the 2 layers of fabric from the pattern. If the pattern is stuck, use pressure and really scrape the paper.

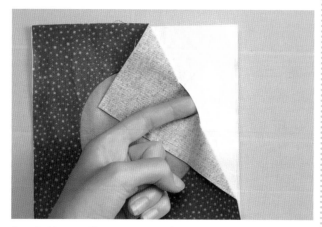

Step 8: Use your finger to remove the pattern

 If you have an area that is not glued when you remove the pattern, use the flower on a flower-head pin to apply a little glue in the area, then iron it dry.

9. Steam iron and then dry iron the circle on a hard surface to make a sharp crease at the fold. The crease forms the sewing line.

 For easy, clean sewing, press until the glue is completely dry.

10. Attach an open-toed or zipper foot to your sewing machine. The clipped seam is on top, extending to the right of the needle. The 1/2" seam allowance provides more fabric for the presser foot to hold onto, allowing it to smoothly follow the curve. Sew 1 thread to the right of the center of the crease. If you find this difficult, see Troubleshooting for tips.

Step 10: Sew.

 Start the stitching away from the crease. At the end of the seam, cross over the first stitches to make a smooth, continuous seam.

11. Trim the seam to ¼". On a soft ironing surface, spray the circle with water, then press the seam in the direction you want it to lie. Pressing the seam toward the circle makes it look like it was appliquéd on top of the background; pressing the seam outward makes the circle look like it was reverse appliquéd into the background.

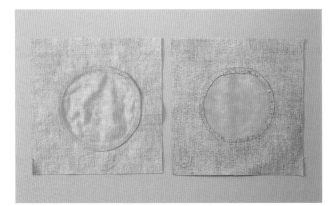

Step 11: Trim and press the seam.

Completed circle

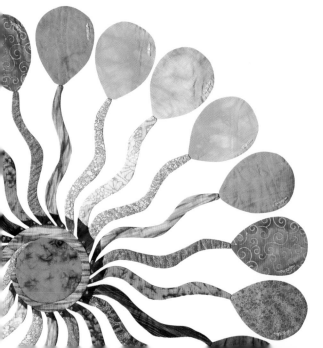

Troubleshooting

If you have trouble seeing the crease when sewing, here are 6 ways to make it more visible:

1. After ironing the pattern to the background fabric (see Step 2), use a contrasting colored pencil to highlight where you need to sew. Make sure your pencil is sharp.

Highlight the circle.

2. In Step 5, make sure you have added enough glue to the folded edge of the tacked seam.

3. In Step 9, spray the circle with water for pressing. Make sure the ironing surface is very firm and that the circle is dry before you sew.

4. Do not pull the fabric too tight in Step 10. You should see a slight hump that creates a shadow.

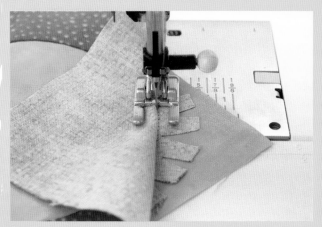

Fabric hump

5. Positioning a light to the left of the sewing machine and shining it at a sharp angle will enhance the shadow even more.

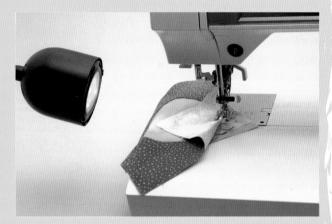

Position a light to the left of your sewing machine.

6. If you are using an open-toed foot, buy an adapter that will allow you to use a generic adjustable zipper foot.

Open-toed feet for Bernina and Pfaff

Singer generic adjustable zipper foot

If your needle position will not go to the outside of the zipper foot, ask a machinist or a person handy with a Dremel tool to trim the outer edge of the foot. I mark these customized feet with dots of red nail polish.

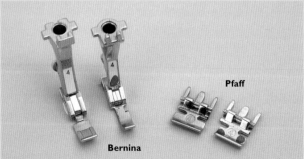

Pfaff

Bernina

Step 6: *Trimmed Bernina and Pfaff zipper feet*

All About Glue

Glue sticks are the key ingredients of Pinless Piecing. There are two options, Avery Removable Glue Stic and Avery Permanent Glue Stic. The removable glue makes removing the pattern incredibly easy, and you can reuse the paper patterns many times. However, there are some limitations. Sometimes the removable glue is not strong enough to tack certain fabrics to the pattern. Some people may not appreciate its odd scent. Also, if the glue is not dry or is applied too heavily, it can make the sewing machine foot sticky, though the glue residue does wash off with soap and water. The removable glue also prevents masking tape from sticking to the pattern, something you will need to do in later projects. I use the removable glue for simple shapes such as circles, and the permanent glue for everything else. Quilters develop their own preferences; find what works best for you.

Of course, I always use the permanent type for gluing the layers of fabric together before sewing. This glue forms a sturdy bond and allows the pieces to be manipulated during sewing.

A QUICK SUMMARY OF PINLESS PIECING

1. Iron the pattern to the back of the fabric.

2. Cut the fabric and clip the seam allowance.

3. Tack the seam to the pattern and iron dry.

4. Glue to the other fabric.

5. Iron dry.

6. Remove the pattern.

7. Steam iron to enhance the crease.

8. Sew in the crease.

9. Trim the seam.

10. Press the seam in a new direction.

Just Circles 2

49" x 58", designed, pieced by Dale Fleming and Dawn Guglielmino; machine quilted by Lee Fowler, 2004.

DESIGN INFORMATION

Dawn Guglielmino and I made this quilt for her son's high school graduation. We created off-kilter Four-Patch blocks in black on white and white on black for a very graphic background. The circle colors, which are pure hues with no subtlety, provide high contrast and energy and communicate wild celebration. For your quilt, feel free to change the dimensions of the circles or the size of the blocks.

FABRIC REQUIREMENTS

FABRIC	AMOUNT	CUT
Background and pieced border	¼ yard each of 10–20 black on white prints ¼ yard each of 10–20 white on black prints	Cut a total of 40 squares 6½" x 6½". Cut a total of 40 squares 6½" x 6½".
Large Circles	⅓ yard each of 7 bright primary colors	Cut a total of 20 squares 9" x 9".
Small Circles	⅓ yard each of 7 bright multicolored prints	Cut a total of 20 squares 9" x 9".
First inner border	¼ yard of black	Cut 5 strips 1¼".
Second inner border and binding	½ yard of red	Cut 5 strips 1½" for border. Cut 6 strips 2" for binding.
Backing	3½ yards	

CONSTRUCTION

1. Sew the 40 black-on-white 6½" squares and 40 white-on-black 6½" squares to make 20 Four-Patch blocks.

2. Skew the ruler and trim the blocks to 9½" x 9½" square.

3. Follow the Six-Minute Circle instructions (page 26) to make 25 freezer paper patterns for circles of all sizes between 3" and 7" diameter. This includes some extra patterns for more variety in the sizes.

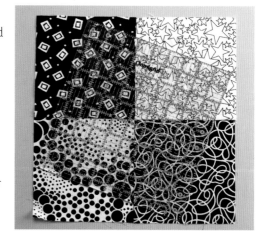

Step 2: *Trim.*

4. Using the patterns with 3″ to 6″ circles, Pinless Piece 20 multicolored circles in primary-color squares. Press the trimmed seam toward the circle.

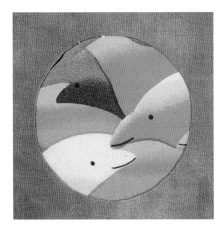

5. Iron the patterns with 5″ to 7″ circles to the back of the Four-Patch blocks, placing some off-center.

6. Pinless Piece (page 26) the primary-color squares with circles to the Four-Patch blocks. Be sure to partially overlap some of the multicolored circles to make them peek out from behind the black-and-white circles. Press the trimmed seams toward the Four-Patch blocks.

Step 6: *Partial circle*

7. Arrange the blocks in a 4 x 5 arrangement on your design wall. Step back and critique your block placement. Do you have "clumps" of color? When you are pleased with the block arrangement, sew the blocks into rows and join the rows.

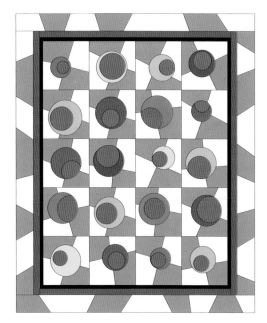

Quilt Assembly Diagram

8. Join the 1¼″ black inner border strips end to end. Measure and cut the border pieces. Add the black borders to the sides, then to the top and bottom of the quilt. Join the 1½″ red inner border strips end to end. Measure and cut the border pieces. Add the red borders to the top and bottom, then to the sides of the quilt.

9. To create the outer border, cut 6″ strips from the leftover black-and-white prints. Cut the ends at various angles and sew together. Trim the borders to 5″ wide and sew to the quilt. Measure and cut the border pieces. Add the outer borders to the sides of the quilt, then to the top and bottom.

Step 9: *Cut strips at angles.*

chapter six

Tips and Cleavage

ALL ABOUT HEARTS

Shapes such as hearts or leaves have angles as well as curves. These angles are more challenging because they require exact needle placement. A tip, or the sharp point at the bottom of a heart, is relatively easy to Pinless Piecing the cleavage, or the point at the top of a heart, is the most challenging skill to learn. I offer three ways to deal with the cleavage shape. I frequently use the tip technique in quilts, but I rarely use the cleavage. I eliminate the need for a cleavage by putting a seam through the point of both positive and negative patterns, creating four shapes instead of two. See the leaves for an example of tips in a quilt. The maple leaves have tips, and the aspen leaves, among others, had the tips eliminated. *Tahoe Blue, Autumn* is shown in its entirety on page 67.

PINLESS PIECING TIPS AND CLEAVAGE

1. Make a heart pattern following the same technique used for circles on page 26. Cut the negative space pattern so it has a smooth edge. If you are using scissors, make the first cut through the positive part of the pattern.

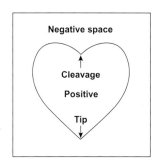

Step 1: Heart pattern

2. Iron the negative space pattern to the back of the background fabric. Cut the fabric, leaving at least a ½" seam allowance.

3. Clip the fabric at the tip to within 2 threads from the pattern. Do not clip the fabric next to the cleavage. Leave the fabric around the point so it looks like a small bib.

4. Tack the clipped edge to the pattern. Notice that at the tip the seam allowance dwindles down to 2 threads.

Steps 3 and 4: Clip and tack.

5. At the cleavage, fold and tack the point with permanent glue. Then fold and tack the left and right sides. Make sure only 1 layer of fabric is at the edge of the pattern.

Step 5: Point

Left

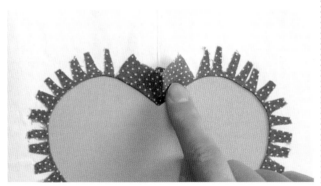

Right

6. Apply glue to the clipped seam, position the background fabric and pattern on the heart fabric, and dry iron.

7. Gently remove the pattern. Keeping the shiny side of the pattern up, slide your fingertip between the pattern and the seam. Be careful with the tip and cleavage. You may need to hold onto the fabric at the tip as you remove the paper.

Step 7: Remove pattern.

Tip **If the seam at the tip or cleavage comes apart when removing the paper, use the flat part of a flower-head pin to add more glue, then iron again.**

8. If the pattern sticks to the fabric at the cleavage, use a dull knife to scrape the fabric away from the pattern.

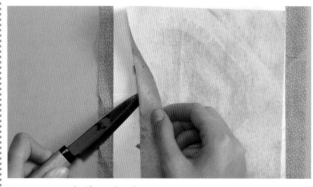

Step 8: Use a knife at the cleavage.

9. From the *front*, place a pin perpendicularly on the last thread at the cleavage. This will enable a more precise clip with your fine-tip scissors.

Step 9: Pin cleavage.

10. From the *back*, clip the fabrics to within 1 thread of the pin. Remove the pin.

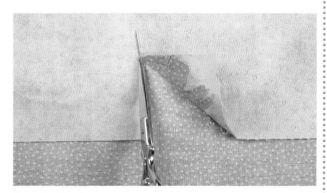

Step 10: Clip cleavage.

11. Use a steam iron to enhance the crease. Starting at the top of the heart, sew to the tip, pivot, and then continue sewing.

Step 11: Turn at the tip.

12. Sew to the cleavage. Stop at the point of the cleavage.

Step 12: Sew to the point.

13. Refold the fabric, pivot, and then continue sewing until the seam is completed. Overlap the stitches.

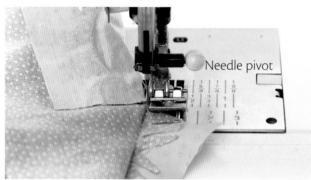

Needle pivot

Step 13: Pivot and sew.

Tip **Put a drop of Dritz Fray Check on a pinhead and rub it on the scant seams at the tip and cleavage. This prevents the glue from spreading and staining the front of the fabric.**

14. Trim the seam to ¼". On a soft ironing surface, spray the heart with water. Press the seam in the direction you want it to lie.

Completed heart

Alternate Cleavage

If you have trouble sewing a cleavage seam that will press inward, here are two alternatives to give the illusion that the heart is on top of the fabric.

Hand appliqué the cleavage point. Many people choose to appliqué because it is efficient when dealing with only a small amount of stitching.

Or, try the following:

1. Make the heart as described in Pinless Piecing Tips and Cleavage, Steps 1–3 (page 34).

2. Tack the fabric as instructed in Step 4. However, leave the seam allowance at the cleavage unfolded and untacked.

3. Apply glue to all edges except the cleavage. Position the pattern and dry iron the background fabric to the heart fabric.

Step 3: *Position and glue.*

4. Remove the pattern. Sew everything except the cleavage.

5. On the back, place the paper heart pattern inside the fabric heart. Line up the edges with the stitching. Dry iron.

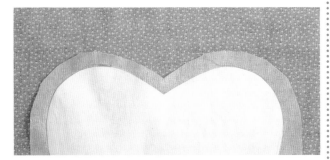

Step 5: *Paper heart at cleavage*

6. Fold, clip, and tack the center heart fabric over the paper heart cleavage. This step turns the cleavage into a tip.

Step 6: *Clip and tack.*

7. Pull the cleavage seam allowance to the back. Glue, then sew the point that has now become a tip. When sewing, cross over the first set of stitching to ensure a continuous line.

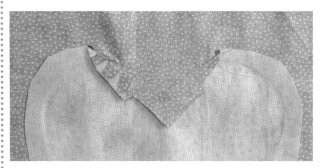

Step 7: *Stitch cleavage seam.*

RINGS AND
SEE-THROUGH HEARTS

Ring

To make a shape that appears to be a ring or see-through heart, sew two of the shapes together with one inside the other. This method works for any shape.

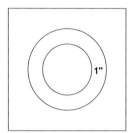

Ring pattern   *Heart pattern*

1. Make a circle (page 26) or heart (page 34). Set aside the background fabric cut from the center.

Step 1: *Make a circle or heart.*

Tip **When making rings, cut out the background of the first circle carefully. The background fabric that is removed becomes the center of the ring, and it needs enough fabric for its own ¹/₂″ seam allowance.**

2. Cut a smaller circle or heart from the positive space patterns. Always make the shapes at least 1″ wide. Place and iron the ring pattern on the back of the first circle.

Step 2: *Place ring pattern on back of first circle.*

3. Clip and tack the seam for the inside circle and place it on the circle of background fabric.

Step 3: *Clip and tack the seam.*

4. Carefully line up the print to create the illusion of a continuous background. Pinless Piece the inside circle or heart.

LINKED RINGS AND HEARTS

Linked rings

The method for making linked objects is the same for any shape.

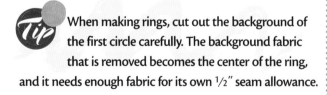

Linked hearts

1. For the linking ring, follow Steps 1-3 for Rings and See-Through Hearts. Position and iron the negative space pattern for another circle. Make sure you leave enough space for the width of your rings, or they will overlap instead of link.

2. Position the pattern over the previously made ring. It will cross over in 2 places. With a seam ripper, open the seam around one overlapped section of the ring. Cut through the other section as you cut out the background. Clip and tack the seam over the rest of the pattern.

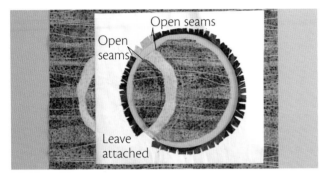

Step 2: Clip and tack.

3. Glue the ring fabric to the circle you just cut. Place the attached fabric out of the way. Pinless Piece the outer edge (see page 26).

Step 3: Sew the second circle.

4. Place the ring pattern on the back of the new circle. Cut, clip, and tack.

Step 4: Ring pattern on back

5. Tuck the edges of the center fabric under the ring.

Step 5: Tuck under the center fabric.

6. Glue and position the background so the print lines up. Pinless Piece the inside circle.

Step 6: Match the print.

7. Appliqué the 2 edges of the original ring where it goes over the new ring. Or, you may Pinless Piece the edges by first cutting away the ring fabric from the back.

Step 7: Appliqué.

To make multiple linked rings or hearts, sew the center ring or heart first, then link the others to it.

Hearts

61″ x 61″, designed and pieced by Dale Fleming; quilted by Lee Fowler, 2004.

DESIGN INFORMATION

It may sound contradictory, but I wanted this quilt to be elegant with a folk-art feel. Although a Mondrian-like grid inspired the composition of the quilt, the hearts are drawn freehand to add an informal touch. I tried to make each heart a little different, as this shape offers many possibilities. The choice of color began with 3 navy/purple fabrics for the background. Because I wanted the hearts to stand out, I chose light-value reds, golds, greens, and blues. Adding a bridging fabric in the block sashing unified the blocks. I only had a small quantity of bridging fabric, not enough to finish the quilt. To extend its use, I bordered it with a dark maroon, which is a darker value of the hearts. The bridging fabric is a Japanese fabric that includes, but does not match, all the colors of the colors used for the hearts and background.

The construction guidelines that follow are suggestions for assembly; let your own quilt evolve as you make the blocks.

MATERIALS
- Basic sewing supplies (page 7)
- Pinless Piecing supplies (page 8)

 FABRIC REQUIREMENTS

FABRIC	AMOUNT	CUT
Background	¾ yard each of 3 solid or textured navy/purple fabrics	
Hearts	½ yard each of 6 prints in light values of blue, pink, gold, green, and peach	
Block borders	1¼ yards of gold print	Cut 6 strips 2½". Cut 11 strips 1½". Cut 2 strips 2".
Sashing and borders	1⅓ yards of burgundy	Cut 12 strips 1¼". Cut 16 strips 1⅝".
	¾ yard of navy print	Cut 6 strips 2". Cut 8 strips 1¼".
Binding	½ yard of navy	Cut 7 strips 2".
Backing	4 yards	

 CONSTRUCTION

1. Make the block backgrounds by cutting and sewing random squares and rectangles. Add 1½" to the block sizes (½" for seams plus 1" extra). Place the pieces on your design wall and critique. If you prefer, use 1 fabric for the background.

2. Design a variety of sizes of free-form hearts. Make double-layered freezer paper patterns (see page 26). With the blue painters' tape and a felt pen, label the back of the block backgrounds and patterns to specify their order, color, the top of the block, and any other information that will keep you organized.

3. Make 10 heart blocks using the Tips and Cleavage techniques (page 34). Sew the heart that looks like it is underneath the others first. On blocks with linking hearts, sew the center heart first. Hearts that appear to be peeking out from behind another are sewn first. Press the trimmed seams toward the hearts.

4. As you make each block, place it on the design wall and critique. If you aren't pleased with a block, don't hesitate to recycle it and learn from the experience.

5. Trim the heart blocks to size, including seam allowances.

6. Border each block with the gold fabric, using 2½" strips on the 2 large blocks, 2" strips on the 13" block, and 1½" strips on the remaining blocks. Vary the sewing order, adding side borders first on some blocks and top and bottom borders first on other blocks.

7. Sew 12 of the burgundy 1¼" strips to 6 of the 2" navy print strips to make sashing A.

8. Sew 16 of the burgundy 1⅝" strips to 8 of the 1¼" navy print strips to make sashing B and the borders.

9. Sew the A and B sashing pieces between the blocks, referring to the quilt assembly diagram. Join the blocks.

10. Sew the borders to the quilt. I added some interest to the corners by sewing a partial seam on the first border piece, then adding the next border piece to that edge. I added the other border pieces, and then finished sewing the first seam.

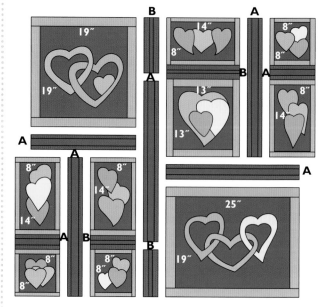

Block dimensions

Suggested Quilt Assembly Diagram

Every Way to Play With Patterns

Traditional quilts are a series of straight-sided shapes put together in some form of grid. Once you leave the straight sides and grid behind, you need a design and pattern to help pull your quilt together. Following are guidelines I use to create my designs and patterns.

Although there are many ways to make patterns, the following method is the simplest and most environmentally friendly; it also works well for my style of quiltmaking.

chapter seven

SUPPLIES

- Pattern Supplies 14–18 (page 8)
- Craft knife
- Paper scissors
- Blue masking tape

DRAWING A DESIGN

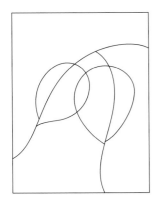

Step 1: *Outlined drawing*

1. Cut vellum to the approximate size of your finished quilt. If the vellum is not wide enough, glue several sheets together. Use a pencil to draw the rough draft. Outline the finished drawing with a fine-point black permanent marker. You may want to erase the pencil lines for a cleaner look and to avoid confusion.

2. If you are unable to make a large drawing, take a small drawing to a copy shop and ask them to enlarge it to the size you want. Then trace it onto the vellum using a permanent marker.

3. To keep track of all the different pieces, label shapes such as "leaf," "hat," and so on with colored pens. Include arrows to indicate the grainline of the fabric or the direction of any stripes.

4. Using a different colored pen, intersect the lines of the drawing. These markings will help you put the elements back together later. Write the word "front" on the side that shows what the finished design will look like.

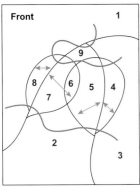

Steps 3 and 4: *Markings*

5. With the back of the vellum facing you, use the blue masking tape to attach the drawing to a large, flat window, or use a lightbox for tracing. On the reverse-image drawing, the word "front" should appear reversed. If you skip this step your final quilt will be a mirror image of your original drawing.

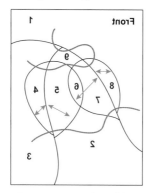

Step 5: Reversed markings

MAKING A PATTERN

1. As for all Pinless Piecing patterns, you need a double layer of freezer paper. To make your pattern larger than 18" wide, iron a top layer of freezer paper at right angles to the bottom layer. Iron from the middle of the freezer paper to the edges to eliminate bubbles. Use a very hot iron so the pieces will adhere to each other. To bond large sheets of freezer paper and keep them flat, collapse the ironing board to floor level. Don't worry if the freezer paper is not perfectly flat or fused; those imperfections will iron out as you use the pattern.

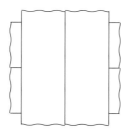

Fuse freezer paper together.

2. Use the blue tape to position the layered freezer paper on top of the drawing on the window or lightbox. Place the shiny side of the freezer paper toward the glass.

3. Trace all of the markings onto the freezer paper. You may want to reverse the numbers and writing so they can be read more easily from the back. The freezer paper pattern should be a mirror image of the original vellum drawing.

How to Use Patterns

Being aware of your personality can help you determine your most efficient quilting style. One notable quilt artist, Ruth McDowell, makes a detailed drawing, selects her fabrics, and then pieces the quilt. At the other end of the spectrum, another gifted artist, Rosemary Eichorn, makes wonderful fabric collages with an idea and fabric but no drawings in between. Most of us are probably somewhere between these two approaches. Every artist develops a way to make patterns for her quilts that complements the way she thinks and sews.

My personal style combines various elements from the two ends of the spectrum. I begin with a basic outline and create units—some with detailed patterns, others as simple strips. Then I move the units around on my design wall until I have a composition that speaks to me. By the time I've finished a quilt, it is often different from what I had first envisioned or designed. I find the transforming process of this evolution absolutely fascinating.

Here are three ways to use patterns:

1. Following a Pattern Exactly

2. Altering a Pattern as You Sew

3. Collage With Multiple Patterns

Incorporate these styles of pattern making into your present method or experiment to develop your own style.

The next three exercises are intended to help you learn a variety of ways to design and make a quilt. If you want to make a quilt, make a fourth block to create the project shown at the end of this chapter. The finished samples are 8½" x 11". Supplies are listed on page 8.

Please note: The convex curves in these patterns are very gentle. If you choose to make sharper convex curves, refer to Fringe Flipping (page 60).

Following a Pattern Exactly

I often use Following a Pattern Exactly for a unit of a quilt rather than an entire quilt. However, *Claire in a Field of Lupines* (page 25) was sewn using only this method.

If you find that this technique works well for you, I recommend any book by Ruth McDowell, a master of this style of quilting. Her books illustrate and explain her design and pattern techniques. Judy Dales is another wonderful artist who creates magical abstract designs and has written an excellent book that demonstrates her exact pattern method.

For this sample, the design and fabric were planned before sewing. You know in advance what the end result will look like.

1. Make a freezer paper pattern, then cut apart the pieces. To keep the pieces in order, pin them on your design board (page 9) next to the vellum drawing as you cut. It may help to turn the vellum over so it looks the same as the cut pattern pieces. (See illustration for vellum drawing and freezer paper pattern below.)

2. Select a fabric and iron the pattern piece to the back. Cut out the fabrics, leaving ½″ to 1″ of fabric around the pattern.

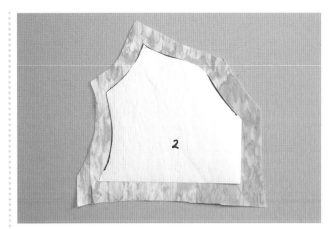

Step 2: *Pattern on fabric*

3. Cut a section at a time, alternating between Steps 1 and 2.

4. Look for logical ways to piece. In this case, sew piece 3 to piece 4 because it makes a nice, smooth curve. If you attempted to sew piece 1 to piece 3, you would have a jagged, impossible shape.

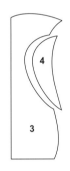
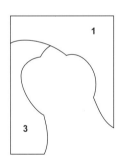

Easy to sew   *Impossible to sew*

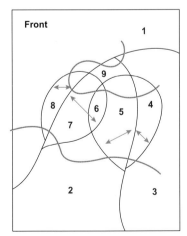

Vellum drawing

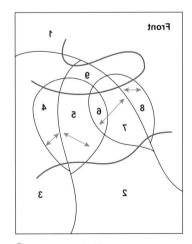

*Freezer paper pattern
(mirror image of vellum drawing)*

Finished sample

5. The easiest curve to sew is a concave curve. If you clipped the edge of the fabric to fold it over the pattern, the seam will be easier to sew with that edge on top. When there is excess fabric on top, you can move it out of the way as you sew. When there is more fabric underneath, it bunches in the seam.

6. To help with positioning, place the pattern piece, shiny side up, on the front of the fabric to which you are gluing a pattern.

***Step 6:** Placement*

7. Pinless Piece (page 26) the smaller shapes into larger units. Sew 1 to 8 and 3 to 4. Sew 6 to 7, lining up the stripes of the fabrics. Sew 9 and 5 to 2. On a unit with several pieces, it is more efficient to glue them all and then sew.

***Step 7:** Building units*

8. Using tan masking tape and the intersecting guidelines, reconstruct your freezer paper pattern piece by piece as you sew. Your pattern should always match your sewn fabric pieces. This will help you assemble your quilt accurately and keep the pieces flat.

9. As you put together the pieces to create units, it may be difficult to keep removing the pattern every time you sew a seam. Instead, fold and pin larger pattern pieces at least 6″ from the area to be sewn. You can mark the fabric with colored pencils to indicate where to replace the pattern.

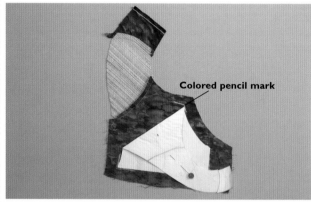

Colored pencil mark

***Step 9:** Fold and pin the pattern (on larger units, the paper would be folded back for ease of sewing).*

10. Press the seams before joining the units. If you want the leaves to appear to be on top, press the seams toward the leaf shapes instead of the background fabric. Use a soft ironing surface and a spray of water. Before sewing over any opposing seams, make sure the seams are pressed in the direction you want.

11. Sew the half-leaf to the middle unit (7/6 to 2/5/9). Sew the side unit (3/4) to the middle unit. Then add the top unit (1/8) to the whole.

12. Trim the block to 9″ x 11½″, which includes seam allowances.

Altering a Pattern as You Sew

Whether for a representation of a particular shape, such as a branch, or just a random design element, adding little slivers of color enlivens quilts. The swooping veins on the leaves of *Tahoe Blue, Autumn* (page 67) were added at this point in the design process even though they were not included in the original drawing or pattern. I don't plan these touches because I am inspired to add details as the quilt develops.

With this method of construction you will have a good idea of the final appearance, although the finished quilt does not match the pattern exactly.

Please note: This pattern has an additional line at the top of the background. (See illustrations below for vellum drawing and freezer paper pattern.)

1. Cut out the pattern and iron it to the fabric as in Following a Pattern Exactly, Steps 1 and 2 (page 45). When you cut the fabric for piece 3, add an extra 1½" of fabric to the inside edge. Trust me on this!

2. Sew together the smaller pieces until you have 4 larger units: 1a, 1/8, 2/5/9/7/6, and 3/4. Follow Steps 3–6 in Following a Pattern Exactly (page 45).

There are three ways to alter a pattern as you sew.

WAYS TO ALTER PATTERNS
Pull Apart

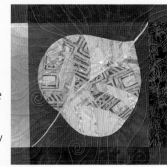

Suppose you want to add a line, representing a twig, between sections 1 and 1a. This is a pull apart. The pattern pieces are pulled apart just enough to show a sliver of another fabric.

1. Fold and tack the fabric over both pattern edges that will border the twig. Cut a piece of twig fabric that will cover the curve plus 2".

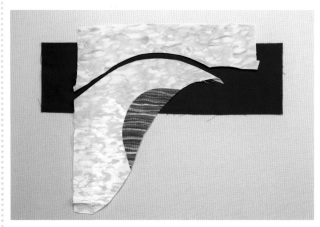

Step 1: *Pull apart.*

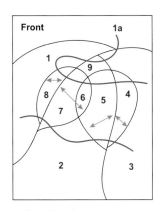

Vellum drawing

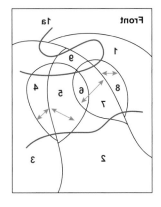

Freezer paper pattern

Finished sample

2. To create an angled end for your twig, glue a folded rectangle of background fabric to the twig fabric.

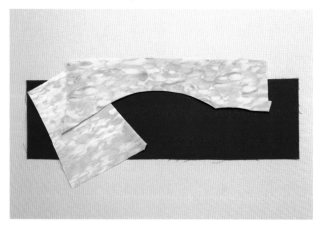

Step 2: Create an angle.

3. Glue the background rectangle, then glue the 2 background pieces to the twig fabric.

4. Highlight the edge of the pattern by running your fingernail on the fabric. Clip the convex curves. Pinless Piece (page 26) the 3 glued seams. Always start with the first fabric that was glued down. After you sew each glued seam, trim it to ¹/₄" before you sew the next seam.

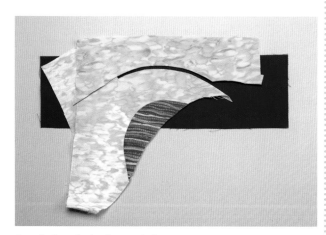

Step 3: Sew the background pieces.

Pull Apart With an Addition

A pull apart changes the curve of the rest of the seam. An addition to the pattern creates a smoother transition or changes a line completely. The three-blade leaf in *Tahoe Blue, Autumn* (page 67) was made this way.

1. The extra fabric you added to piece 3 allows you to make an addition. Add extra freezer paper to unit 3/4 to extend your pattern on the new line. Iron the freezer paper pieces together, then trim.

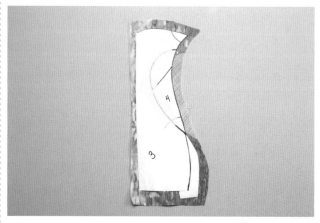

Step 1: Add to the pattern.

2. Iron the modified pattern 3/4 to the back of your fabric and prepare for Pinless Piecing (page 26). Prepare the middle unit (2/5/6/7/9) for Pinless Piecing. As before, cut the twig fabric to cover the curve plus 2".

3. By placing the new unit 3/4 on top of the middle unit, the seam will curve more.

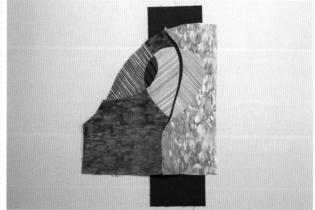

Step 3: Addition on top of middle unit

By placing the new unit 3/4 under the middle unit, the seam will curve less.

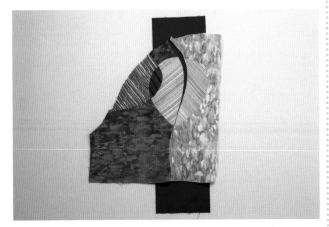

Step 3: Addition under middle unit

4. Position and piece the units to create the desired curved seam. Remember: The first seam glued is the first seam sewn.

Pull Apart With a New Cut

Sometimes when you pull two pattern pieces apart, particularly with an S curve, you don't get quite the shape you desire.

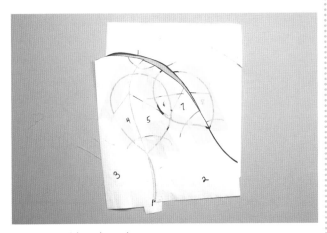

Pull apart with awkward curve

1. On the large units, cut off a sliver of the pattern between the adjoining pieces to create a new line.

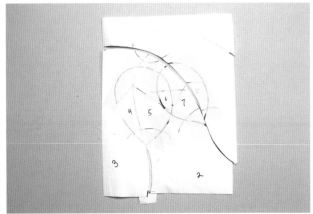

Step 1: Cut pattern.

2. Pinless Piece (page 26) the units to the twig fabric.

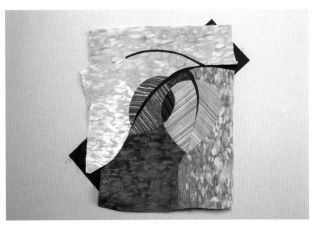

Step 2: Sew new line.

3. Trim the block to 9″ x 11½″, which includes seam allowances.

Collage With Multiple Patterns

Although it may seem that you are wasting fabric and time by creating a full background, this method gives you the most flexibility in your finished design, makes for an easier final assembly, and, as a bonus, makes your quilt lie flat. All projects in this book feature an element of collage.

Even in the first project, the size and placement of the circles could and did change as the quilt evolved. Jane Sassaman, author of *The Quilted Garden*, works in a collage style.

As with the previous two methods, make patterns from the vellum drawing. In this case, make one pattern of just the background and a second set of patterns of the leaves. The area around the leaves will serve as negative space patterns.

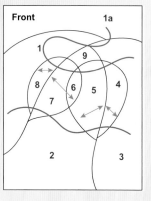

Vellum drawing

Background freezer paper pattern

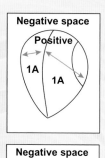

Finished sample

Leaf patterns

1. Create the background by either Following a Pattern Exactly, Altering as You Sew, or a combination of these methods. The sample demonstrates the Altering a Pattern as You Sew method.

2. Create the leaf units. Use the positive space pattern and the Altering a Pattern as You Sew method to add stems. You may want to add shadows or "moth holes." Make 3 leaves.

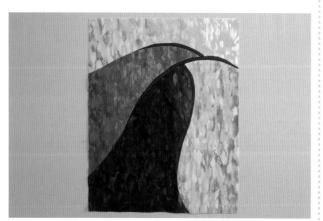

Step 1: *Finished background*

Step 2: *Leaf units*

Tip Moth holes are small Six-Minute Circles (page 26). Use the background fabric in the holes to add a more lifelike appearance.

3. Reconstruct the positive patterns for the leaves. Iron the patterns to the back of the fabric leaves. Fold and lightly tack the seams to the back of the pattern. This gluing is temporary but will help you design your collage.

Step 3: Tack leaf units.

4. Place the leaves on the background where you want them. Consider design elements such as balance and symmetry. Avoid placing a tip or cleavage on a seam. Outline the leaves with glass head pins inserted straight into the fabric and design board.

Step 4: Positioning leaf units

5. Turn the background fabric over and use the pinpoints as guidelines to position the appropriate negative space pattern.

6. Cut, clip, and tack the background fabric. See Pinless Piecing Tips and Cleavage (page 34) for a review of tips and cleavage, if necessary.

Tip Folding seams over the edge of the freezer paper sometimes makes lumps. Cut a small notch in the freezer paper for the seam to lie flat.

Step 6: Negative space pattern placement with joins showing

7. Remove the pattern from the back of the leaf and iron the leaf flat. Position and Pinless Piece the leaf. Spray with water and iron the seam toward the leaf to give it a raised look. Repeat with the other leaves.

8. Trim the block to 9″ x 11½″, which includes seam allowances.

Overlapping Patterns

When a design has many positive space shapes that you want to place exactly, use a technique I refer to as Overlapping Patterns. *Tuscan Sunflowers* and *Spiro Giro* (page 63), and the maple and oak leaves in *Tahoe Blue, Autumn* (page 67) were

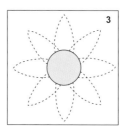

made with Overlapping Patterns. Rather than making eight separate patterns for the sunflower petals in *Tuscan Sunflowers*, only two patterns were required.

For this sunflower example, make three overlapping patterns; two for petals and one for the sunflower center. These are negative space patterns.

1. Make a vellum design.

2. Stack 3 double-layered freezer paper sheets with the shiny sides all facing up. Place the vellum drawing on top with the front facing up. Staple the layers together. Avoid

Vellum design

stapling over the drawn lines. Remove all thread from your sewing machine, including the bobbin. Needle-draw the pattern by stitching on the lines.

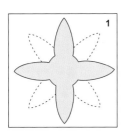

3. Remove the staples and number the patterns 1, 2, and 3.

4. On pattern 1 cut the center circle and every other petal.

Step 4: Cut center and petals.

5. Place pattern 1 on top of pattern 2. With a felt-tip pen mark the openings where the paper has been removed from pattern 1. Now cut all the unmarked petals and the center.

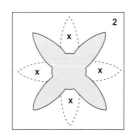

Step 5: Cut circle and unmarked petals.

6. On pattern 3, cut the center circle only.

Step 6: Cut circle.

7. Iron pattern 1 to the background fabric. Cut and clip the fabric. Tack only the petal seams. Glue to the petal pieces.

Step 7: Prepare the petal seams.

8. Pinless Piece (page 26) the first 4 petals. Trim and press the seams toward the petals.

Step 8: Pinless Piece the first petals.

9. Position pattern 2 so the petals are placed between the petals from pattern 1. Notice how they overlap. Because of sewing irregularities your finished seams will not match the pattern exactly. Pinless Piece the remaining petals. Trim and press the seams toward the petals.

Step 9: Position pattern 2

10. Position pattern 3 so it overlaps the ends of the petals. Pinless Piece the center. Trim and press the seams toward the center.

Tuscan Sunflowers, 68" x 82", designed and pieced by Diana Mehrmann, Hong Kong; machine quilted by Victoria Simpson and Michelle Lingo, Galt, California, 2003.

On one of Diana's quick trips through the United States, we had time for a half-hour lesson on circles, tips, and patterns. Using 2 alternating patterns for the petals and one pattern for the centers, Diana designed these lovely sunflowers using colors traditionally associated with Tuscany, Italy.

To Leaf

29" x 29", designed, pieced, and quilted by Dale Fleming, 2004.

DESIGN INFORMATION

To Leaf drew inspiration from the quilt *Tahoe Blue, Autumn* and my friend Angie Woolman's fascination with leaves. Add one more block to the three practice blocks you made in Every Way to Play With Patterns (page 43) and you will have a quilt!

 FABRIC REQUIREMENTS

FABRIC	AMOUNT	CUT
Background and borders	2 fat quarters sky colors ½ yard each of 2 blues	Cut 2 strips 3½" from each ½-yard piece.
Leaves	¼ yard each of 4 striped fabrics, plus small scraps	
Twigs	1 fat quarter of brown	
Block borders	¼ yard of purple	Cut 5 strips 1".
Sashing and center square	¼ yard each of 2 analogous oranges, plus scrap of another orange	Cut 2 strips 1" from each of two fabrics. From the third, cut 1 square 3½" x 3½".
Binding	⅓ yard	Cut 4 strips 2".
Backing	1 yard	

 CONSTRUCTION

1. Make 4 blocks using the Every Way to Play With Patterns techniques (page 43) (or make only 1 if you already made the samples from this chapter). I chose to add 2 of the leaves from the Collage block to my first 2 blocks, and then I made 1 more block using the Following a Pattern Exactly method.

2. Trim the blocks to 9" x 11½", which includes seam allowances. If you trimmed too much, add a strip of "sky" fabric.

3. Border the blocks with 1" purple strips. Sew the strips to the sides, then to the top and bottom.

4. Sew a 1" analogous orange strip to the bottom of each rectangular block.

5. Arrange the blocks around the 3½" orange square. Join the square to one of the blocks by sewing a partial seam.

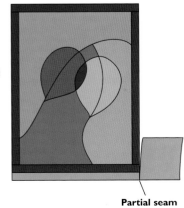

Partial seam

MATERIALS

- Basic sewing supplies (page 7)

- Pinless Piecing supplies (page 8)

- Pattern supplies (page 8)

6. Sew the next block to the square and first block. Add the other 2 blocks. Finish sewing the rest of the first seam.

7. Measure and cut the inner border pieces from the 1″ light and dark orange strips. Join light and dark orange pieces to make the top border. Sew to the top, lining up the seam with the block seam. Add a dark orange piece to the bottom edge. Add a light orange piece to the left side and a dark orange piece to the right side.

8. Measure and cut the outer border pieces from the 3½″ light and dark blue strips. Add a light blue 3½″ piece to the left side. Join light and dark blue pieces to make the top border. Sew to the top, lining up the seam with the inner border seam. Add dark blue pieces to the right side and the bottom edge.

Quilt Assembly Diagram

Sinuous Curves

I love the rhythm and movement of curves—ripples in water, swaying trees. Although I have always wanted to put these curves in my quilts, I never cared for the tedious piecing that was required.

Knowing how to sew a good-looking curve enhances your ability to design your dream quilt. Curves are important for making the background texture for a quilt, assembling sections, constructing collages, and matching print lines from one fabric to the next.

The most impressive part of The Sinuous Curves technique is the speed with which these curves can be created. Choosing the fabric and designing the pattern takes longer than the actual sewing. It took me two days to sew *Handel's Water Music* (page 61), while the background for *Identity Crisis* (page 74) took only an afternoon using the Sinuous Curves technique.

The traditional method for creating gentle curves is to cut two overlapping fabrics and sew the pieces together with the right sides together. However, this cut-and-sew technique is very limited in its applications. If you want more precision or if the curves are tight, Pinless Piecing works best. Using a sewing machine with an adjustable zipper foot or with an adjustable needle (a needle that can be moved to the right or left) is easier and faster than using an open-toed foot. If your machine only uses an open-toed foot, use Fringe Flipping (page 60) for the convex curves.

chapter eight

Sailboats, 66" x 54", designed and pieced by Dale Fleming; machine quilted by Lee Fowler, 2003.

PINLESS PIECING SINUOUS CURVES WITH UNMATCHED FABRIC

Creating curves without matching the prints of the fabric is easy and fast. It's a great way to add curves to a quilt, like the waves in the water of *Sailboats* and the curved sections in *Mondrian Waves* (page 69).

1. Draw a curved design and make a pattern from double-layered freezer paper.

2. Iron the patterns to the wrong side of your chosen fabrics. Cut the fabrics, leaving at least a ½" seam allowance on all sides. Prepare 1 side of the curved edges (either all top or all bottom edges) of the pieces for Pinless Piecing (page 26).

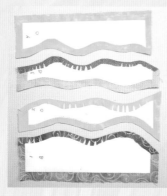

Step 2: Prepare the edges.

3. From the front, make an indentation in the fabric by running your fingernail along the untacked edges of the pattern. Use the indentations to position the pieces. Place the pattern for the last piece on top to position it correctly. Glue the pieces in position.

Step 3: Position and glue the pieces.

4. Remove the patterns, placing your fingertip between the pattern and the seam, with the pattern shiny side up. If you find yourself peeling individual sections of clipped seam from the pattern, you have the wrong side facing up.

5. Steam iron, and sew the seam using Pinless Piecing. If necessary, use Fringe Flipping on convex curves (page 60). The first seam glued will be the first one sewn. Trim and press the seam allowance after each stitching.

PINLESS PIECING SINUOUS CURVES WITH MATCHED FABRIC

To make a sample of this technique you will need a print fabric in 2 colorways.

1. To match the designs of 2 fabrics, lay out the larger piece. Place the smaller piece on top and match the prints. Cut the fabrics so they are the size of your pattern, plus 1" all around. The extra inches are your fudge factor.

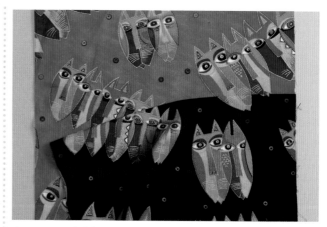

Step 1: Match fabric prints.

2. Draw a curved design and make a double-layered freezer paper pattern. Label the sections you want to be positive space patterns or negative space patterns. Number the pieces. Add a wavy line in another color to help you line up the pattern pieces.

3. Cut apart the pattern pieces, then reassemble and iron them to the back of one of the fabrics.

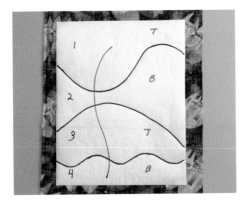

Step 3: Cut and iron.

4. Remove the pattern pieces that represent the second fabric. In this example, remove the positive space pieces (turquoise).

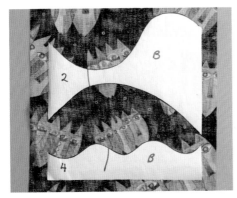

Step 4: Remove pattern pieces.

5. Cut the first fabric (black), leaving at least a ½″ seam allowance on all sides. Clip and tack the fabric over the curved edges of the pattern.

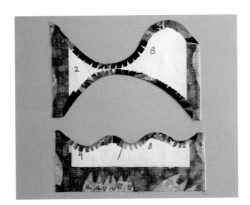

Step 5: Prepare units.

6. Place the turquoise fabric on your work surface with the right side up. Position the black pieces on top. Match the lines of the fabric designs, using the positive space pattern for assistance. Use pins to mark the lines that need to be matched exactly. Fabric stretches, so tug and adjust the fabric to get everything lined up correctly.

Remove the pieces, apply permanent glue to the edges (be generous), and, using the pins for guidance, reposition. Press with a dry iron.

Step 6: Position and glue.

7. From the back, make an indentation at the edge of the pattern by running your fingernail along the glued edge. Cut at least ½″ from this line. Where the piece is narrow, do not cut too close to the opposite edge. Clip where needed.

8. Remove the pattern by placing your fingertip between the pattern and the seam, with the pattern shiny side up. If you find yourself peeling the clipped seam from the pattern, you have the wrong side facing up.

9. Steam iron and sew the seam. Trim seams to ¼″ and iron the seam in the direction you prefer. Use the Fringe Flipping method (page 60) if you are using an open-toed foot.

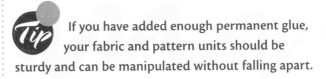 If you have added enough permanent glue, your fabric and pattern units should be sturdy and can be manipulated without falling apart.

Fringe Flipping: Open-Toed Foot Instructions

Sometimes a convex curve is difficult to sew because the bottom layer of fabric keeps bunching under the sewing machine foot. Using a zipper foot, with the needle placed to the left of the foot, helps to avoid this problem. If you use a different foot, such as an open-toed foot, Fringe Flipping helps deal with challenging curves. Because both seam allowances are clipped, the seam is a fringe; flipping it turns convex curves into concave curves.

1. After the pieces of either matched or unmatched fabrics are steamironed, make an indentation on the back by running your finger along the glued edge of the pieces. Use a contrasting colored pencil to further highlight the edge.

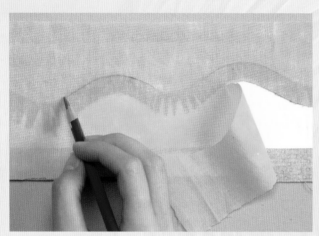

Step 1: Pencil highlight

2. Clip the seam so it can flip in the opposite direction. Iron, then steam to form a sharp crease.

Step 2: Flip the fringe.

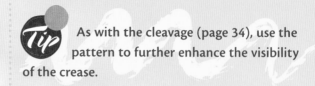

Tip As with the cleavage (page 34), use the pattern to further enhance the visibility of the crease.

3. Sew the flipped seam in the new crease. Try to sew in the middle of the pencil line.

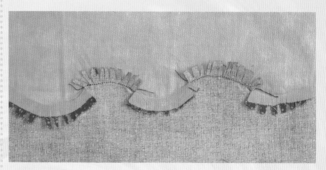

Step 3: Sew.

4. After sewing the flipped seams, steam and iron them back to the original position. Sew the concave seams, overlapping the ends of the previous stitching.

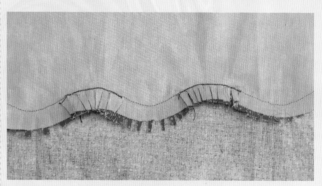

Step 4: Finish sewing.

Handel's Water Music

51" x 45", designed, pieced, and quilted by Dale Fleming, 2003.

DESIGN INFORMATION

In *Handel's Water Music* the curves are my interpretation of the four movements of a symphony. To create your own rhythm and movement quilt, put on your favorite music and draw what you hear.

I bought these fabrics years ago, but I didn't have the skills to make the quilt until I figured out my Sinuous Curves method. For your quilt, look for a print that is available in two or more colorways. When manufacturers print fabric they usually print each design in at least four colorways. Designers offer so many choices in patterns and colors that I'm sure you will find a fabric that inspires you.

FABRIC REQUIREMENTS

FABRIC	AMOUNT	CUT
Background	1 yard of one colorway 1 yard plus 1 repeat of the pattern in a second colorway	
Grasses	1 yard of bright olive green	
First border	1/3 yard of orange	Cut 5 strips 1½".
Second border	1/4 yard of bright olive green	Cut 5 strips 3/4".
Outer border	3/4 yard of blue	Cut 5 strips 4".
Binding	1/2 yard of light blue	Cut 6 strips 2".
Backing	3 yards	

 # CONSTRUCTION

1. Design and make the patterns for a Sinuous Curves background. Match and Pinless Piece the 2 fabrics using Sinuous Curves (page 58). Refer to Fringe Flipping (page 60) if necessary.

2. Design the foreground grasses. If they are not at least 1" wide, they will be a challenge to sew. As you did with the leaves in Collage With Multiple Patterns (page 50), use positive space patterns for positioning and negative space patterns for piecing.

3. Pinless Piece the grasses to the background.

4. Square your quilt top to 41" x 35" plus seam allowances.

5. Join the 1¹⁄₂″ orange inner border strips end to end. Measure and cut the border pieces. Add the orange borders to the sides, then to the top and bottom of the quilt. Join the ³⁄₄″ green inner border strips end to end. Measure and cut the border pieces. Add the green borders to the top and bottom, then to the sides of the quilt. Join the 4″ blue outer border strips end to end. Measure and cut the border pieces. Add the blue outer borders to the sides, then to the top and bottom of the quilt.

Quilt Assembly Diagram

Spiro Giro, 42″ x 37″, Lee Fowler, Portland, Oregon, 2004.

Lee was inspired by a piece of antique Art Deco jewelry and had her fabrics dyed specifically for her work. Notice how the colors of the jewel play off the negative space and how the quilting enhances the design to make the whole quilt sparkle.

chapter nine

Unpaper Piecing

Many quilters dislike foundation piecing because of the difficulties involved with transferring a pattern to the foundation fabric. Paper piecing can be problematic because the removal of the paper from the finished piece is very tedious and invariably weakens the stitching. Therefore, I have created a method that I call Unpaper Piecing, which uses fusible interfacing, and represents a cross between the two. As in paper piecing, multiple patterns can be made at once, but unlike foundation piecing, the backing is not removed and the stitching is protected. When the quilt is finished, the interfacing foundation is invisible.

Unpaper Piecing may be used to solve several sewing challenges. Most artists use it when precision piecing is needed, because it creates very precise points. In addition, this technique may be used to produce multiple identical patterns. I also use this method with silk, loosely woven fabrics, or fabrics of different weights because the interfacing stabilizes the different materials.

PATTERNS ON FUSIBLE INTERFACING

Patterns can be applied to the interfacing in two ways.

One-of-a-Kind Patterns

For *Mondrian Waves* (page 69), different one-of-a-kind patterns were used, just as was done for the corona around the face on *Hot Flash* (page 73). To make one-of-a-kind patterns, use a microtip permanent marker and a ruler. Draw your design without seam allowances on the nonfusible side of the interfacing.

Remember, your completed design will be a mirror image of what you drew.

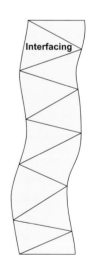

One-of-a-kind pattern

Fruit Wedgie, 43" x 43", designed, pieced, and quilted by Denise Killingsworth, Walnut Creek, California, 2004.

Although the lines of this quilt's blocks are basically the same, Denise plays with the colors. The same basic fabrics appear in each block but in different quantities, and her use of green and magenta makes the piece vibrate with energy. Even with all its diversity, her quilt has great unity.

Identical Patterns

Use this method to make all of your strips with the same pattern. *Stellar* (page 72), *Carnival* (page 67), and *Fruit Wedgie* relied on this method. This is the same needle-drawing technique used for Overlapping Patterns (page 52).

1. Most projects will require 1 freezer paper pattern and several identical interfacing patterns of your choice. Draw your pattern without seam allowances on the freezer paper. Cut the interfacing the same size as the freezer paper patterns.

2. Stack the freezer paper and the interfacing pieces with the plastic coating and fusible dots all facing down. Staple the layers together. Your finished unit will be the mirror image of what you drew.

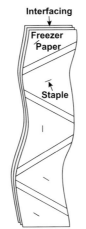

Step 2: Stack and staple

3. Insert the wing needle in your sewing machine and stitch on the drawn lines to needle-draw the pattern.

4. Remove the staples. If you cannot see the perforations well enough to sew on them, place the interfacing on a dark surface and, with a microtip pen and ruler, draw the lines.

5. Use the pattern as you would for foundation or paper piecing.

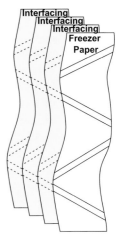

Step 3: Needle-draw

 I often make a freezer paper pattern first, even for a one-of-a-kind pattern. Drawing the design on freezer paper allows you to erase mistakes, and then you can use the freezer paper as a template to cut fabric for the block.

UNPAPER PIECING

 Tip To prevent the fusible interfacing from sticking to your ironing board, use parchment paper or Teflon sheets.

1. Make your interfacing patterns, using either the one-of-a-kind or identical patterns (page 64) methods.

2. Unpaper Piecing follows classic paper or foundation piecing techniques, with frequent ironing. Cut strips of fabric that will generously cover the shapes drawn on the interfacing.

3. Place the first fabric right side down on the ironing board. Position the fusible interfacing on top of the fabric with the fusible side down. Position the sewing line on the straight edge of the fabric. Press with a medium-hot iron. Make sure the fabric extends at least ¹/₂″ beyond the edge for the seam allowance. Caution: Do not iron over the perforations or they will disappear.

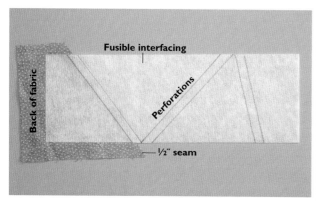

Step 3: Fabric placement

4. Place the second fabric right side up on your work surface. Position the interfacing strip on top with the right sides of the fabrics together. Make sure the fabric will easily cover the pattern and the ¹/₂″ outside seam allowance.

5. Pin along the seam and stitch on the perforated line.

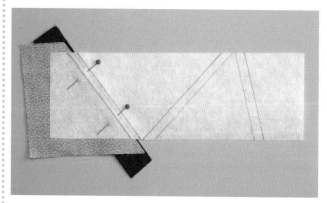

Steps 4 and 5: Place, pin, and stitch.

6. Flip open the fabric and iron from the right side. Avoid ironing glue side of the interfacing.

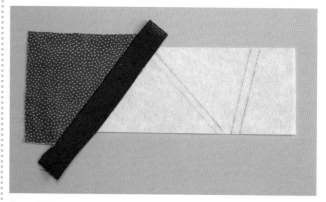

Step 6: Iron.

7. Repeat Steps 4–6 until the strip is finished.

 Tip When ironing on fusible interfacing, always keep the temperature of your iron at medium.

Do not use steam for the initial ironing. Once you steam, the interfacing is fused.

Iron just to the perforations, not over them, or the holes will disappear.

Do not iron on the glue (bumpy) side of the interfacing.

Carnival, 69" x 87", designed, pieced, and quilted by Margaret Rice, Alamo, California, 2002.

Margaret, who has a marvelous sense of color, combines unusual color combinations and fabrics from all over the world to create quilts with stunning effects. She also took a class in the Evolving Blocks method using Unpaper Piecing. Carnival is her interpretation of the celebration prior to Lent. Notice that the eye finds no rest in this joyous work; but then, there is no rest during carnival either!

String Piecing the Unpaper Way

String Piecing includes many variations, and every quilter has her own favorite method. Like stripping, String Piecing creates a textured fabric, but because the fabrics are sewn at an angle, a lot of visual motion is created. I use this method mostly to create background texture. The quilt *Tahoe Blue, Autumn* uses this method in its pastel background.

Tahoe Blue, Autumn, 63" x 70", designed and pieced by Dale Fleming; machine quilted by Lee Fowler, 2003.

California's Lake Tahoe in autumn inspired this quilt. Both the mountain sky and the jewel-toned lake possess every shade and variation of blue. The leaves were quick to make. I used every technique described in this book for construction of this quilt.

String Piecing

1. Cut fusible interfacing to the size of your finished unit. If the design is curved, cut a freezer paper pattern as well.

2. Place the interfacing on the first fabric piece, making sure the fabric extends past the edge of the interfacing by at least ¹/₂". Fuse the fabric to the interfacing.

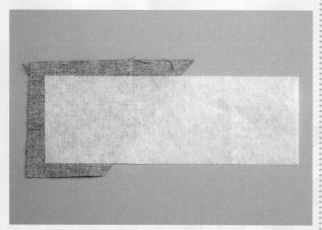

Step 2

3. Place the second piece on top of the first, right sides together. Note the angle. Make sure that when the piece is flipped to the right side there will be at least ¹/₂" extra for the seam allowance on the sides.

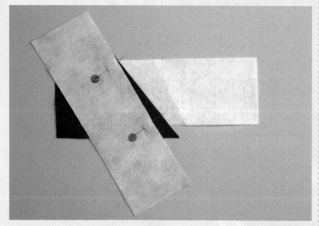

Step 3

4. Sew on the straight edge of the second fabric.

5. Trim the first fabric to a ¹/₄" seam allowance. Flip open the fabric and iron from the right side. Avoid ironing on the glue in the interfacing. Trim the outside to a ¹/₂" seam allowance.

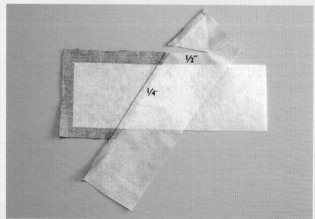

Step 5

6. Repeat Steps 3–5 until the strip is covered, changing the angle each time.

Step 6

7. When trimming your finished strip, measure and cut it to the proper size rather than just trimming ¹/₄" past the edge of the interfacing.

Mondrian Waves

49" x 61", designed, pieced, and quilted by Jane Beatty, Brentwood, California, 2003.

MATERIALS

- Basic sewing supplies (page 7)
- Pinless Piecing supplies (page 8)
- Pattern supplies (page 8)
- Unpaper Piecing supplies (page 9)

 ## DESIGN INFORMATION

Jane Beatty is an accomplished quilter who loves precision. In this quilt, she used the Evolving Blocks method while exploring related designs and colors in different strips. Each strip has a pattern based on the idea of triangles, and the color palette spans the entire color wheel. The background fabric—a light-value, dull yellow batik with bright hints of coral and lime—draws attention to the other colors and adds subtlety. Long, gentle curves placed asymmetrically on the quilt demonstrate the Mondrian-inspired pattern. Even if the undulating strips were straight, which would be easier for a beginner, the rhythm and movement of the piece would be maintained. The orange inner border highlights the warm colors, and the darkest blue in the border provides a complementary color to the orange. The soft colors and subtle designs are like a beautiful morning sunrise. This quilt expresses the tranquility before excitement begins.

Mondrian Waves demonstrates how to use Pinless Piecing with other techniques. Although in this case, Pinless Piecing is combined with Unpaper Piecing, it could just as easily be raw edge appliqué, ribbon work, or anything else. Sandy Cummings, a wonderful quilt artist, explores many ways of combining innovative techniques in her book *Thinking Outside the Block*. Remember: Methods are made to be mixed.

FABRIC REQUIREMENTS

FABRIC	AMOUNT	CUT
Background	1½ yards of main color and ½ yard of secondary color	
Pieced strips	Small pieces of 40 different light and dark fabrics that do not blend into the background color	
Inner border	¼ yard of red	Cut 5 strips 1".
Outer border	1½ yards of blue	Cut 4 strips 6½" on the lengthwise grain
Binding	½ yard of blue	Cut 6 strips 2".
Backing	3 yards	
Interfacing	4 yards	Cut 2 pieces 54" long.

 CONSTRUCTION

1. Make freezer paper and interfacing patterns for each strip. Cover the ironing surface with parchment paper. Place a piece of interfacing with the fusible side down, then place the freezer paper with the shiny side down. With a medium-hot iron, lightly iron the freezer paper to the interfacing. From the fused pieces, cut 6 long wavy strips, varying in width from 3″ to 5″. The sample has two 3″ strips, one 3¹/₂″ strip, two 4″ strips, and one 5″ strip.

If you are making identical patterns, stack and needle-draw your designs (see page 65). If not, remove the freezer paper and draw your design with a microtip pen on the interfacing.

2. Use Unpaper Piecing (page 66) or String Piecing (page 68) to make the strips.

3. Iron the corresponding freezer paper pattern to the interfacing strips. Fold and tack the seam allowances to the side edges.

Step 3: *Tack unit.*

4. Choose the size of the finished background. The size of the sample is 36″ x 48″. Add 3″ to the dimensions and cut the main background to that measurement. Pin to your design board.

5. Place your pieced strips in the pattern or rhythm you prefer. Take your time. Shoot digital or Polaroid pictures of the patterns you like best.

6. Use ¹/₈″ or ¹/₄″ quilters' tape to outline the strip placement. Follow the lines to make repositioning easy. Add any notes with blue tape.

Step 6: *Outline the strips with masking tape.*

7. Place the second background fabric on top of the main background. Pin in place. Outline the strip placement with masking tape. Cut the second background piece with 1″ seams all around.

Step 7: *Change the background.*

8. Where 1 strip goes underneath another, cut the end of the strip, allowing a 1″ seam.

9. Glue the strips to the background fabrics. In the areas where you changed the background, glue to the second fabric, and then cut away the main background behind it. Your goal is to have a flat quilt!

10. Pinless Piece (page 26) the strips to the background fabrics. Refer to Collage With Multiple Patterns (page 50) and Sinuous Curves (page 58) for positioning and sewing the strips. Sew partial seams as needed. Add the adjacent pieces, then finish the partial seam.

11. Square the quilt top to 36" x 48" plus seam allowances.

12. Join the 1" red inner border strips end to end. Measure and cut the border pieces. Add the red borders to the top and bottom, then to the sides of the quilt. Measure and cut the 6½" blue outer border pieces. Add the blue borders to the sides, then the top and bottom of the quilt.

Quilt Assembly Diagram

Stellar, 81" x 81", designed, machine pieced, and quilted by Jane Beatty, 2003.

All Together Now

The real fun begins here. Because you now have the skills to sew anything you can imagine, you can explore shapes in your quilting that you never thought possible. Remember, the mantra should be to use any method that makes piecing easier. Please notice how each skill you have learned has the flexibility to be used many different ways. In this project, overlapping patterns and identical patterns have been combined for a slightly different method in the construction of the wings. The Sinuous Curves method (page 58) was tweaked. There are many more creative ways to use these methods; tweak them and try.

Hot Flash, Dale Fleming, 35″ x 42″, 2002.

I completed the background and border for Hot Flash in a class, then I created the face by following a pattern exactly. I used Unpaper Piecing (page 66) with a one-of-a-kind only pattern for the corona. The four rings and head units are affixed to the background using Collage (page 50). In choosing fabric for this quilt, I had little regard for the actual color and designed instead for warm/cool and value.

Identity Crisis

49" x 49", designed, pieced and quilted by Dale Fleming, 2004.

DESIGN INFORMATION

Identity Crisis responds to the question: "Can you imagine what a shock it must be for a caterpillar to suddenly discover it has wings?" This quilt took four days to sew.

The inspiration for this quilt was the trunk of a huge old oak tree, including the deep crevices in the bark. The background fabrics are therefore a combination of warm muted browns, cool greens, blues, and purples, with a lot of light values. Although monarch butterflies usually have only two or three shades of orange, the butterfly in this quilt has twelve fabrics—a bright analogous mix of yellows to reds. Choosing the fabrics for this quilt took longer than the actual sewing.

Because this is a collage quilt, the butterfly wings should be made first to determine the size of the background. The butterfly can be enlarged to any size. To copy the design to freezer paper, use the methods of constructing a drawing and a pattern (see page 43). Feel free to change the design in any way or to design your own butterfly. Before you cut your pattern, practice making smaller circles. Change the sizes or eliminate, appliqué, or embroider the smallest circles. The background is made using Sinuous Curves (page 58), though the pieces are closer together and sometimes overlap. Good alternate background methods include String Piecing (page 68), as in *Tahoe Blue, Autumn* (page 67), or stripping (page 23), as in *Hot Flash* (page 73). The butterfly's body is three overlapping ovals set in the background. The wings are identical freezer paper patterns, using many of the Overlapping Patterns techniques (see page 52). The independent wing units are set into the background using Collage With Multiple Patterns (page 50).

MATERIALS

- Basic sewing supplies (page 7)
- Pinless Piecing supplies (page 8)
- Pattern supplies (page 8)

FABRIC REQUIREMENTS

FABRIC	AMOUNT	CUT
Background	1 yard each of 8 fabrics that remind you of bark; 3 should be very light values	
Wings	1 yard of black	
Spots on wings	Scraps of 12 very bright yellow to red prints and solids	
Wing edges and body	1/2 yard each of 3 prints with white dots on black	
First border	1/4 yard of black	Cut 4 strips 1 1/4".
Second border	1/4 yard of red-orange	Cut 4 strips 1".
Third border	1/3 yard of color-base neutral with as many colors of the quilt as possible	Cut 4 strips 2".
Outer border	3/4 yard of textured black	Cut 5 strips 4 1/2".
Binding	1/2 yard of black	Cut 5 strips 2".
Backing	3 yards of a fabric you love!	

CONSTRUCTION

1. Make an 18″ x 36″ vellum drawing. To ensure symmetry, fold the vellum in half. Draw 1 wing on 1 side and then trace the second wing from the first, including construction information. Although you use only 1 wing, draw both so you can see the design balance.

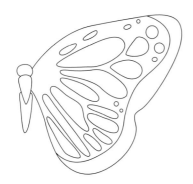

Half of pattern: Enlarge to approximately 18″.

Pattern with mirror image added for second wing

2. Iron 12 sheets of freezer paper together to make 6 identical 18″ x 20″ patterns for the wings. Since you need mirror images, stack 3 freezer paper sheets with the shiny sides facing up, and 3 freezer paper sheets with the shiny sides facing down. Place the vellum drawing on top. Staple, and use a dull Jeans needle to needle-draw the pattern. If your sewing machine will not "sew" that many layers of paper, needle-draw the left and right sides separately. Make sure they are mirror images. Trim excess paper surrounding the positive space wing pattern.

3. Number the patterns left 1 to 3 and right 1 to 3.

4. Working with both left and right patterns, cut out as many of the openings for the wing spots in pattern 1 as you can. Do not cut adjacent spots. Keep at least ½″ of paper between any cutouts.

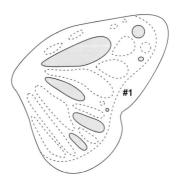

Step 4: Cut out openings.

5. Place pattern 1 on pattern 2 and mark which wing spots were cut. Now cut out as many of the remaining openings as possible, keeping at least ½″ of paper between them.

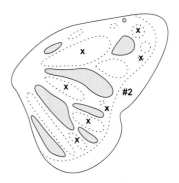

Step 5: Mark and cut.

6. Place patterns 1 and 2 on pattern 3 and mark which wing spots were cut. Cut the remaining holes.

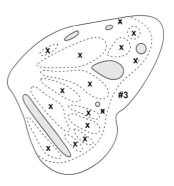

Step 6: Cut remaining holes.

7. Iron left and right pattern 1 to the back of 2 pieces of black fabric. Trim the fabric at least 1" larger than the pattern.

8. Pinless Piece (page 26) of the cutouts on pattern 1.

9. Repeat Step 8 for pattern 2 and 3.

10. Cut the pattern for the curved edge of the wing from pattern 1 or 2.

11. Iron to the dotted fabric and prepare the inner edge for Pinless Piecing.

12. Use pattern 3 to position the curved edge. Pinless Piece using the Sinuous Curves technique (page 58).

13. Lightly tack the wing fabric over the pattern edge, as described in positioning leaves in Collage With Multiple Patterns (page 50).

14. Put both wings on your design wall and decide how much background you want around your butterfly. Add 5" extra to both the width and the height. In the example, 31" x 31" is expanded to 36" x 36".

MAKING THE BACKGROUND

1. Iron 8 sheets of freezer paper together to make 4 pattern sheets 40" x 18" (or larger, if you chose to have more background).

2. Cut 25 long pieces with 1 straight side and 1 curved side approximately 4" wide. Make some curves deeper than others. I added some shorter half-moon shapes for interest.

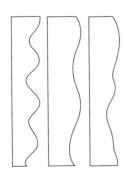

Background curves

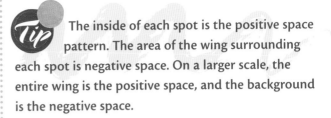

The inside of each spot is the positive space pattern. The area of the wing surrounding each spot is negative space. On a larger scale, the entire wing is the positive space, and the background is the negative space.

3. Spread the strips, shiny side up, on a table or the floor. Move them around and overlap them until you have a combination that appeals to you. Remember that you have extra length, so move the pieces vertically as well as horizontally. The example uses 17 strips.

4. Place your uncut background fabrics on the design wall, then place your 2 wings on top to make sure you have enough contrast in both value and color. Stand back and critique.

5. Iron the patterns to the fabrics in the same order. Cut the background fabrics, allowing 1/2" seams on the curved edges and 1" to 5" extra on the straight edges, depending on your design. Tack the fabrics over the curved edges of the patterns.

6. Spread the curved strips on a table or floor. Move them around and overlap them until you have a combination that appeals to you. Simultaneous contrast will change the proportions from your original design. Place the butterfly wings on your pattern to make sure the design still works.

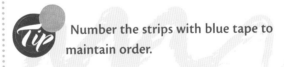

Number the strips with blue tape to maintain order.

7. If you choose, make a tracing of the pattern pieces or take a photo of the composition. (I usually just wing it.)

8. As in Pinless Piecing Sinuous Curves With Unmatched Fabrics (page 58), glue all the curved edges and then sew. Remember: The first pieces glued down are the first seams sewn.

COLLAGING THE BUTTERFLY

1. Make the patterns for the butterfly body. Make a positive and negative space pattern each for the head, thorax, and abdomen.

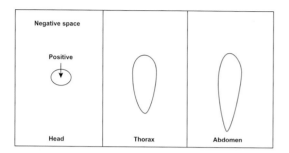

Body patterns

2. Cut the fabrics for the body pieces. Lightly tack the fabrics to the patterns, as described in Collage With Multiple Patterns (page 50).

3. Position the wings with the body pieces on top. If your background is heavily textured, the little pieces of the body may disappear. Arrange the butterfly until there is better contrast. Remove the body pieces before marking the positions of the wings with pins. Glue the wings to the background.

4. Dry the glue with an iron. From the back, use your fingernail to trace around the edge of the wing pattern. Use this indentation as a guide for cutting the excess background fabric from behind the wing. Pinless Piece (page 26) the wings.

5. Position the body pieces and outline the head and abdomen with pins. Use the pins to position the negative space patterns. Remove the head and abdomen pieces from the patterns and press flat. Pinless Piece. Position and Pinless Piece the thorax.

FINISHING

1. Square up the quilt top to 36″ x 36″ plus seam allowances.

2. Measure and cut the 1¼″ black inner borders. Add the black borders to the sides, then to the top and bottom of the quilt. Measure and cut the 1″ red inner border pieces. Add the red borders to the sides, then to the top and bottom of the quilt. Measure and cut the 2″ color-base inner borders. Add to the sides, then to the top and bottom of the quilt.

3. Measure the quilt top and add 4″ (the finished width of the outer border). Sew the 4½″ textured black strips end to end and cut 4 border pieces to that measurement. Sew a partial seam joining the side of a border piece to a corner of the quilt. Sew the next border piece to the end of the first border and the quilt. Add the other 2 border pieces. Finish sewing the first partial seam. This treatment adds interest to the quilt.

*A Round Down Under,
57″ x 57″, designed, pieced, and quilted
by Dale Fleming, 2003.*

This quilt was constructed using all the methods in this book. It is a study in simultaneous contrast in colors that I rarely use, with many tones and shades. The circles are Sinuous Curves altered with collaged strips. The outside rings of the circles were altered as they were sewn, and the final setting of the circles used Collage With Multiple Patterns (page 50).

A FINAL WORD

When I first contemplated writing this book, I envisioned several pages of instructional how-tos and the majority of pages dedicated to color and design. If it only takes six minutes to show someone how to Pinless Piece a Six-Minute Circle, it seemed logical that it would only take a few pages to explain it. However, everyone I talked to had questions about what else could be done with Pinless Piecing, and so those few pages of instruction grew to include far more. In the end, I had a book on quilting techniques.

These techniques can be liberating for many experienced quilters while still simple enough for novices to master. As you incorporate Pinless Piecing into other methods with which you are already familiar, let the methods influence one another. If you like embellishing with ribbons, combine this technique with Pinless Piecing. Use these techniques as starting points to enhance your own work and expand your horizons.

Just There, 40" x 40", designed, pieced, and quilted by Vicki Wind, Pleasant Hill, California, 2003.

ABOUT THE AUTHOR

Dale Fleming enjoys teaching and loves to see quilters discover new ways to quilt and expand their vision. She believes she learns as much from her students as they do from her. Her quilts have been shown in both regional shows and larger venues, including the Pacific International Quilt Show, Houston International Quilt Show, Quilt National, and Visions. Although her quilts appear to have many styles, all explore the same ideas: the interplay of movement, light, and color. She is most interested in how each element interacts with and draws from others and yet retains its individuality.

When Dale is not quilting, she can be found in her garden, creating combinations of form and color with flowers, which then appear in her quilts. Her other passion is cooking, and many people will testify that she makes killer chocolate truffles.

Dale lives in Walnut Creek, California, with her husband, Jerry, who is very supportive of her artistic endeavors. They have two children, Emily and Nicholas. You can see Dale's quilts at www.dalefleming.com.

BIBLIOGRAPHY

The following books from my library relate to the substance of this book. However, everything relating to color in this book came from what I learned in Laverne Edwards's color class.

Art Books

Bois, Yve-Alain, Joop Joosten, Angelica Zander Rudenstine, and Hans Janssen, *Piet Mondrian*, New York: Little, Brown and Co., 1995.

Bridget Riley, Moorhouse, Paul, ed, Millbank, London: Tate Publishing, 2003.

Design Books

De Grandis, Luigina, *Theory and Use of Color*, New York: Harry N. Adams, Inc.,1986.

Itten, Johannes, *The Art Of Color*, New York: Van Nostrand Reinhold, 1973.

Lauer, David A., *Design Basics*,Wadsworthy/Thompson Learning Academic Resource Center: Australia, 2002.

Oei, Loan, *The Elements of Design*, New York: Thames and Hudson Inc., 2002.

Shibukawa, Ikuyoshi, *Designers' Guide to Color 1-5*, San Francisco: Chronicle Books, 1990.

Stoops, Jack, *Design Dialogue*, Worcester, MA: Davis Publications, Inc., 1990.

Quilt Books

Brackman, Barbara, *Encyclopedia of Pieced Quilt Patterns*, Paducah, KY: American Quilters Society, 1993.

C&T Publishing, *All About Quilting From A to Z*, Lafayette, CA: C&T Publishing, 2002.

Cummings, Sandy, *Thinking Outside the Block*, Lafayette, CA: C&T Publishing, 2004.

Dales, Judy, *Curves in Motion*, Lafayette, CA: C&T Publishing,1998.

Eichorn, Rosemary, *The Art of Fabric Collage*, Newtown, CT: Taunton Press, 2003.

Johnston, Ann, *The Quilters' Book of Design*, Lincolnwood, IL: The Quilt Digest Press, 2000.

McClun, Diana, and Laura Nownes, *Quilts! Quilts!! Quilts!!!*, Lincolnwood, IL: The Quilt Digest Press, 1997.

McDowell, Ruth, *Art and Inspirations*, Lafayette, CA: C&T Publishing, 1996.

McDowell, Ruth, *Symmetry*, Lafayette, CA: C&T Publishing, 1994.

Ringle, Weeks, *Color Harmony for Quilts*, Gloucester, MA: Rockport, 2002.

Sassaman, Jane, *The Quilted Garden*, Lafayette, CA: C&T Publishing, 2000.

Wolfrom, Joan, *The Visual Dance*, Lafayette, CA: C&T Publishing, 1995.

INDEX